I0670979

AUNT RACHEL

DAVID CHRISTIE MURRAY

Aunt Rachel

David Christie Murray

© 1st World Library, 2009
PO Box 2211
Fairfield, IA 52556
www.1stworldlibrary.com
First Edition

LCCN: 2009923373

Softcover ISBN: 978-1-4218-8822-4
Hardcover ISBN: 978-1-4218-8921-4
eBook ISBN: 978-1-4218-8723-4

Purchase *"Aunt Rachel"*
as a traditional bound book at:
www.1stWorldLibrary.com/purchase.asp?ISBN=978-1-4218-8822-4

1st World Library is a literary, educational organization
dedicated to:

- Creating a free internet library of downloadable ebooks

- Hosting writing competitions and offering book publishing
scholarships.

Interested in more 1st World Library books? contact:
literacy@1stworldlibrary.com

Check us out at: www.1stworldlibrary.com

1st World Library Literary Society

Giving Back to the World

"If you want to work on the core problem, it's early school literacy."

- James Barksdale, former CEO of Netscape

"No skill is more crucial to the future of a child, or to a democratic and prosperous society, than literacy."

- Los Angeles Times

"Literacy... means far more than learning how to read and write... The aim is to transmit... knowledge and promote social participation."

- UNESCO

"Literacy is not a luxury, it is a right and a responsibility. If our world is to meet the challenges of the twenty-first century we must harness the energy and creativity of all our citizens."

- President Bill Clinton

"Parents should be encouraged to read to their children, and teachers should be equipped with all available techniques for teaching literacy, so the varying needs and capacities of individual kids can be taken into account."

- Hugh Mackay

PREFACE

A critic, otherwise almost altogether friendly, protests, in reviewing a recent book of mine, that no rustics ever would, could, or will talk in real life as the rustics in that work are made to talk by me. Since this criticism might apply still more pointedly, if it were true, to "Aunt Rachel" than to "Rainbow Gold," I desire to say a word or two in self-defence. A little, a very little, of the average rustic would go a long way in fiction. But I do not profess to deal with the average rustic. I deal, and love to deal, with the rustic exceptional, the village notable and wiseacre. Observant readers will have noticed that the date of one story is 1853, and that the epoch of the other is remoter by a dozen years. In my boyhood, in the Staffordshire Black Country, the rustic people were saturated with the speech of the Bible, the Church Service, and the "Pilgrim's Progress." It is otherwise to-day, and their English, when it pretends at all to a literary flavor, is the English of the local weekly paper. The gravity, the slow sententiousness, and purposed wisdom of the utterances of more than one or two knots of habitual companions whom I can recall, were outside the chances of exaggeration. Often these people were really wise and witty. They were the makers of the local proverbial philosophy, and many of their phrases are alive today. I recall and could set down here a score of the quaintest bits of humor and good-sense, and one or two things genuinely poetical, which were spoken in my childish hearing. But I refrain myself easily from this temptation, because I have not written my last Black Country story, and prefer to put these things in a form as near their own as I can achieve. I only desire to say that I have *not* exaggerated, but have fallen short of the characteristics I have had to deal with.

D. Christie Murray.

Rochefort, Belgium, December, 1885.

CHAPTER I

A quartette party—three violins and a 'cello—sat in summer evening weather in a garden. This garden was full of bloom and odor, and was shut in by high walls of ripe old brick. Here and there were large-sized plaster casts—Venus, Minerva, Mercury, a goat-hoofed Pan with his pipes, a Silence with a finger at her lips. They were all sylvan green and crumbled with exposure to the weather, so that, in spite of cheapness, they gave the place a certain Old-world and stately aspect to an observer who was disposed to think so and did not care to look at them too curiously. A square deal table with bare top and painted legs was set on the grass-plot beneath a gnarled apple-tree whose branches were thick with green fruit, and the quartette party sat about this table, each player with his music spread out before him on a portable little folding stand.

Three of the players were old, stout, gray, and spectacled. The fourth was young and handsome, with dreamy gray-blue eyes and a mass of chestnut-colored hair. There was an audience of two—an old man and a girl. The old man stood at the back of the chair of the youngest player, turning his music for him, and beating time with one foot upon the grass. The girl, with twined fingers, leaned both palms on the trunk of the apple-tree, and reposed a clear-colored cheek on her rounded arm, looking downward with a listening air. The youngest player never glanced at the sheets which the old man so assiduously turned for him, but looked straight forward at the girl, his eyes brightening or dreaming at the music. The three seniors ploughed away business-like, with intent frownings, and the man who played the 'cello counted beneath his breath, "One, two, three, four—one, two, three, four," inhaling his breath on one set of figures and blowing on the next.

The movement closed, and the three seniors looked at each other like men who were satisfied with themselves and their companions.

"Lads," said the man with the 'cello, in a fat and comfortable voice, "that was proper! He's a pretty writer, this here Beethoven. Rewben, the hallygro's a twister, I can tell thee. Thee hadst better grease thy elbow afore we start on it. Ruth, fetch a jug o' beer, theer's a good wench. I'm as dry as Bill Duke. Thee canst do a drop, 'Saiah, *I* know."

"Why, yes," returned the second-fiddle. "Theer's a warmish bit afore us, and it's well to have summat to work on."

The girl moved away slowly, her fingers still knitted and her palms turned to the ground. An inward-looking smile, called up by the music, lingered in her eyes, which were of a warm, soft brown.

"Reuben," said the second-fiddle, "thee hast thy uncle's method all over. I could shut my eyes an' think as I was five-and-twenty 'ear younger, and as he was a-playin'. Dost note the tone, Sennacherib?"

"Note it?" said the third senior. "It's theer to be noted. Our 'Saiah's got it drove into him somehow, as he's the one in Heydon Hay as God A'mighty's gi'en a pair of ears to."

8   David Christie Murray

"An' our Sennacherib," retorted Isaiah, "is the one as carries Natur's license t' offer the rough side of his tongue to everybody."

"I know it's a compliment," said the younger man, "to say I have my uncle's hand, though I never heard my uncle play."

"No, lad," said the old man who stood behind his chair. "Thee'rt a finer player than ever I was. If I'd played as well as thee I might have held on at it, though even then it ud ha' gone a bit agen the grain."

"Agen the grain?" asked the 'cello-player, in his cheery voice. "With a tone like that? Why, I mek bold to tell you, Mr. Gold, as theer is not a hammer-chewer on the fiddle, not for thirty or may be forty mile around, as has a tone to name in the same day with Rewben."

"There's a deal in what you say, Mr. Fuller," said the old man, who had a bearing of sad and gentle dignity, and gave, in a curious and not easily explainable way, the idea that he spoke but seldom and was something of a recluse. "There's a deal in what you say, Mr. Fuller, but the fiddle is not a thing as can be played like any ordinary instryment. A fiddle's like a wife, in a way of speaking. You must offer her all you've got. If she catches you going about after other women—"

"It's woe betide you!" Sennacherib interrupted.

"You drive her heart away," the old man pursued. "The fiddle's jealouser than a woman. It wants the whole of a man. If Reuben was to settle down to it twelve hours a day, I make no doubt he'd be a player in a few years' time."

"Twelve hours a day!" cried Sennacherib. "D'ye think as life was gi'en to us to pass it all away a scrapin' catgut?"

"Why, no, Mr. Eld," the old man answered, smilingly. "But to my mind there's only two or three men in the world at any particular space o' given time as has the power gi'en 'em by Nature to be fiddlers; that is to say, as has all the qualities to be masters of the instryment. It is so ordered as the best of qualities must be practised to be perfect, and howsoever a man may be qualified to begin with, he must work hour by hour and day by day for years afore he plays the fiddle."

"I look upon any such doctrine as a sinful crime," said Sennacherib. "The fiddle is a recrehation, and was gi'en us for that end. So, in a way, for them as likes it, is skittles. So is marvils, or kite-flyin', or kiss-i'-the-ring. But to talk of a man sittin' on his hinder end, and draggin' rosined hosshair across catgut hour by hour and day by day for 'ears, is a doctrine as I should like to hear Parson Hales's opinion on, if ever it was to get broached afore him."

"Ruth," called the 'cello-player, as the girl reappeared, bearing a tray with a huge jug and glasses, "come along with the beer. And when we've had a drink, lads, well have a cut at the hallygro. It's marked 'vivaysy,' Reuben, an' it'll tek thee all thy time to get the twirls and twiddles i' the right placen."

Ruth poured out a glass of beer for each of the players, and, having set the tray and jug upon the grass, took up her former place and position by the apple-tree.

"Wheer's your rosin, 'Saiah?" asked Sennacherib.

"I forgot to bring it wi' me," said Isaiah. "I took it out of the case last night, and was that neglectful as I forgot to put it back again."

"My blessid!" cried Sennacherib, "I niver see such a man!"

"Well, well!" said the 'cello-player, "here's a bit. You seem to ha' forgot your own."

"What's that got to do wi' it?" Sennacherib demanded. "I shall live to learn as two blacks mek a white by-an'-by, I reckon. There niver was a party o' four but there was three wooden heads among 'em." The girl glanced over her arm, and looked with dancing eyes at the youngest of the party. He, feeling Sennacherib's eye upon him, contrived to keep a grave face. The host gave the word and the four set to work, Reuben playing with genuine fire, and his companions sawing away with a dogged precision which made them agreeable enough to listen to, but droll to look at. Ruth, with her chin upon her dimpled arm, watched Reuben as he played. He had tossed back his chestnut mane of hair rather proudly as he tucked his violin beneath his chin, and had looked round on his three seniors with the air of a master as he held his bow poised in readiness to descend upon the strings. His short upper lip and full lower lip came together firmly, his brows straightened, and his nostrils contracted a little. Ruth admired him demurely, and he gave her ample opportunity, for this time he kept his eyes upon the text. She watched him to the last stroke of the bow, and then, shifting her glance, met the grave, fixed look of the old man who stood behind his chair. At this, conscious of the fashion in which her last five minutes had been passed, she blushed, and to carry this off with as good a grace as might be, she began to applaud with both hands.

"Bravo, father! bravo! Capital, Mr. Eld! capital!"

"Theer," said Sennacherib, ignoring the compliment, and scowling in a sort of dogged triumph at the placid old man behind Reuben's chair, "d'ye think as *that* could be beat if we spent forty 'ear at it? Theer wa'n't a fause note from start to finish, and time was kep' like a clock."

"It's a warmish bit o' work, that hallygro," said old Fuller, in milder self-gratulation, as he disposed his 'cello between his knees, and mopped his bald forehead. "A warmish bit o' work it is."

"Come, now," said Sennacherib, "d'ye think as it could be beat? A civil answer to a civil question is no more than a beggar's rights, and no less than a king's obligingness."

"It was wonderful well played, Mr. Eld," the old man answered.

"Beat!" said Isaiah. "Why it stands to natur' as it could be beat. D'ye think Paganyni couldn't play a better second fiddle than I can?"

"Ought to play second fiddle pretty well thyself," returned Sennacherib. "Hast been at it all thy life. Ever since thee was married, annyway."

"Come, come, come," said the fat 'cello-player. "Harmony, lads, harmony! How was it, Mr. Gold, as you come to give up the music. Theer's them as is entitled to speak, and has lived i' the parish longer than I have, as holds you up to have been a real noble player."

"There's them," the old man answered, "as would think the parish church the finest buildin' i' the king-dom. But they wouldn't be them as had seen the glories of Lichfield cathedral."

"I'm speakin' after them as thinks they have a right to talk," said the other.

"I might at my best day have come pretty nigh to Reuben," the old man allowed, "though I never was his equal. But as for a real noble player—"

"Well, well," said Fuller, "it ain't a hammer-chewer in a county as plays like Reuben. Give Mr. Gold a chair, Ruth. I should like to hear what might ha' made a man throw it over as had iver got as far."

"I heard Paganini," the old man answered. "I was up in London rather better than six-and-twenty year ago, and I heard Paganini."

"Well?" asked Fuller.

"That's all the story," said the old man, seating himself in the chair the girl had brought him. "I never cared to touch a bow again."

"I don't seem to follow you, Mr. Gold."

"I have never been a wine-drinker," said Gold, "but I may speak of wine to make clear my mean-in'. If you had been drinkin' a wonderful fine glass of port or sherry wine, you wouldn't try to take the taste out of your mouth with varjuice."

"I've tasted both," said the 'cello-player, "but they niver sp'iled my mouth for a glass of honest beer."

"I can listen to middlin'-class music now," said Gold, "and find a pleasure in it. But for a time I could not bring myself to take any sort of joy in music. You think it foolish? Well, perhaps it was. I am not careful to defend it, gentlemen, and it may happen that I might not if I tried. But that was how I came to give up the fiddle. He was a wonder of the world, was Paganini. He was no more like a common man than his fiddlin' was like common fiddlin'. There was things he played that made the blood run cold all down the back, and laid a sort of terror on you."

"I felt like that at the 'Hallelujah' first time I heerd it," said Isaiah. "Band an' chorus of a hundred. It was when they opened the big Wesley Chapel at Barfield twenty 'ear ago."

"We'll tek a turn at Haydn now, lads," said the host, genially.

"I'm sorry to break the party up so soon," Reuben answered, "but I must go. There are people come to tea at father's, and I was blamed for coming away at all. I promised to get back early and give them a tune or two." He arose, and, taking his violin-case from the grass, wiped it carefully all over with his pocket-handkerchief. "I was bade to ask you, sir, if Miss Ruth might come and pass an hour or two. My mother would be particularly pleased to see her, I was to say."

The young fellow was blushing fierily as he spoke, but no one noticed this except the girl.

"Go up, my gell, and spend an hour or two," said her father. "Reuben 'll squire thee home again."

"Wait while I put on my bonnet," she said, as she ran past Reuben into the house. Reuben blushed a little deeper yet, and knelt over his violin-case on the grass, where he swaddled the instrument as if it had been a baby, and bestowed it in its place with unusual care and solicitude.

"Reuben," said his uncle, as the young man arose, "that's a thing as never should be done." The young man looked inquiry. "The poor thing's screwed up to pitch," the old man explained, almost sternly. "Ease her down, lad, ease her down. The strain upon a fiddle is a thing too little thought upon. You get a couple o' strong men one o' these days, and

David Christie Murray

make 'em pull at a set of strings, and see if they'll get them up to concert pitch! I doubt if they'd do it, lad, or anything like. And there's all that strain on a frail shell like that. I've ached to think of it, many a time. A man who carries a weight about all day puts it off to go to bed." "Wondrous delicate an' powerful thing," said old Fuller. "Reminds you o' some o' them delicate-lookin' women as'll goo through wi' a lot more in the way o' pain-bearin' than iver a man wool."

"Rubbidge!" said Sennacherib. "You'd think the women bear a lot. They mek a outcry, to be sure, but theer's a lot more chatter than work about a woman's sufferin', just as theer is about everythin' else her does. Dost remember what the vicar said last Sunday was a wick? It 'ud be a crime, he said, to think as the Lord made the things as is lower in the scale o' natur' than we be to feel like us. The lower the scale the less the feelin'. Stands to rayson, that does. I mek no manner of a doubt as he's got Scripter for it."

"Lower in the scale of natur', Mr. Eld?" said Gold, turning his ascetic face and mournful eyes upon Sennacherib.

"Theer's two things," returned Sennacherib, "as a man o' sense has no particular liking to. He'll niver ask to have his cabbage twice b'iled, nor plain words twice spoke. I said 'Lower in the scale o' na-tur'.' Mek the most on it."

Sennacherib was short but burly, and between him and Gold there was very much the sort of contrast which exists between a mastiff and a deer-hound.

"I will not make the most of it, Mr. Eld," the old man said, with a transient smile. "I might think poorlier of you than I've a right to if I did. When a rose is held lower in the scale of natur' than a turnip, or the mastership in music is gi'en in again the fiddle in favor o' the hurdy-gurdy, I'll begin to think as you and me is better specimens of natur's handiwork than this here gracious bit o' sweetness as is coming towards us at this minute. Good-evenin', Mr. Eld. Good-evenin', Isaiah. Good-evenin', Mr. Fuller. Good-evenin', Reuben. No, I'm not goin' thy way, lad. Call o' me to-morrow; I've a thing to speak of. Good-evenin', Miss Ruth."

When he had spoken his last good-by he folded his gaunt hands behind him and walked away slowly, his shoulders rounded with an habitual stoop and his eyes upon the ground. Ruth and Reuben followed, and the three seniors reseated themselves, and each with one consent reached out his hand to his tumbler.

"Theer's a kind of a mildness o' natur' in Ezra Gold," said Isaiah, passing the back of his hand across his lips, "as gives me a curious sort o' likin' for him."

"Theer's a kind of a mildness o' natur' in a crab-apple," said Sennacherib, "as sets my teeth on edge."

"Come, come, lads, harmony!" said Fuller. He laid hold of his great waistcoat with the palms of both hands and agitated it gently. "It beats me," he said, "to think of his layin' by the music in that way, and for sich a cause."

"Well," said Sennacherib, "I'll tell thee why he laid by the music. I wonder at Gold settlin' up to git over men like me with a stoory so onlikely."

"What was it, then?" asked Isaiah, bestowing a wink on Fuller.

"It was a wench as did it," said Sennacherib. "He was allays a man as took his time to think about a thing. If he'd been a farmer he'd ha' turned the odds about and about wi' regards to gettin' his seed into the ground till somebody 'ud ha' told him it 'ud be Christmas-day next Monday. He behaved i' that way wi' regards to matrimony. He put off thinkin' on it till he was nigh on forty—six-an'-thirty he was at the lowest. Even when he seemed to ha' made up what mind he'd got he'd goo and fiddle to the wench instead o' courtin' her like a Christian, or sometimes the wench 'ud mek a visit to his mother, and then he'd fiddle to her at hum. He made eyes at her for all the parish to see, and the young woman waited most tynacious. But when her had been fiddled at for three or four 'ear, her begun to see as her was under no sort o' peril o' losin' her maiden name with Ezra. So her walked theer an' then—made up her mind an' walked at once—went into some foreign part of the country to see if her couldn't find somebody theer as'd fancy a nice-lookin' wench, and tek less time to find out what he'd took a likin' for."

"Was that it?" asked Isaiah, with the manner of a man who finds an explanation for an old puzzle. "That 'ud be Rachel Blythe."

"A quick eye our 'Saiah's got," said Sennacherib. "He can see a hole through a ladder when somebody's polished his glasses. Rachel Blythe was the wench's name. Her was a little slip of a creator', no higher than a well-grown gell o' twelve, but pretty in a sort o' way."

"Why, Jabez, lad," cried Isaiah, "thee lookest like a stuck pig. What's the matter?"

The host's eyes were rounded with astonishment, and he was staring from one of his guests to the other with an air of fatuous wonder.

"Why," said he, with an emphasis of astonishment which seemed not altogether in keeping with so simple a discovery, "this here Rachel Blythe was my first wife's second cousin. Our Fanny Jane used to be talkin' about her constant. Her had offers by the baker's dozen, so it seemed, but her could never be brought to marry. Fanny Jane was a woman as was gi'en a good deal up to sentiment, and her was used to say the gell's heart was fixed on somebody at Heydon Hay. It 'ud seem to come in wi' the probability of things as they might have had a sort of a shortness betwixt 'em, and parted."

"Theer was nobody after her here but Ezra Gold," said Sennacherib. "Nobody. I niver heard, howsever, as they got to be hintimate enough to quarrel. But as for Paganyni, that's rubbidge. The man played regular till Rachel Blythe left the parish, and then he stopped."

"Well, well," said the host, contemplatively, "it's too late in life for both on 'em. Her's back again. Made us a visit yesterday. Her's took that little cottage o' Mother Duke's on the Barfield Road."

"Bless my soul!" said Isaiah. "I seen her yesterday as I was takin' my walks abroad. But, Jabez, lad, her's as withered as a chip! The littlest, wizen-edest, tiniest little old woman as ever I set eyes on. Dear me! dear me! To think as six-an'-twenty 'ear should mek such a difference. Her gi'en me a nod and a smile as I went by, but I niver guessed as it was Rachel Blythe."

"Rachel Blythe it was, though," returned old Fuller. "Well, well! To think as her and Mr. Gold should ha' kep' single one for another. Here's a bit of a treeho, lads, as I bought in Brummagem the day afore yesterday. It's by that new chap as wrote 'Elijah' for the festival. Let's see. What's his name again? Mendelssohn. Shall us have a try at it?"

CHAPTER II

The Earl of Barfield stood at the lodge gate on a summer afternoon attired in a wondrously old-fashioned suit of white kerseymere and a peaked cap. He was a withered old gentleman, with red-rimmed eyes, broad cheek-bones, and a projecting chin. He had a very sharp nose, and his close-cropped hair was of a harsh, sandy tone and texture. He was altogether a rather ferret-like old man, but he had, nevertheless, a certain air of dignity and breeding which forbade the least observant to take him for anything but a gentleman. His clothes, otherwise spotless, were disfigured by a trail of snuff which ran lightly along all projecting wrinkles from his right knee to his right shoulder. This trail was accentuated in the region of his right-hand waistcoat pocket, where his lordship kept his snuff loose for convenience' sake. He was over eighty, and his head nodded and shook involuntarily with the palsy of old age, but his figure was still fairly upright, and seemed to promise an activity unusual for his years. He rested one hand on the rung of a ladder which leaned against the wall beside him, and glanced up and down the road with an air of impatience. On the ground at his feet lay a billhook and a hand-saw, and once or twice he stirred these with his foot, or made a movement with his disengaged right hand as if he were using one of them.

When he had stood there some ten minutes in growing

impatience, a young gentleman came sauntering down the drive smoking a cigar. Times change, and nowadays a young man attired after his fashion would be laughable, but for his day he looked all over like a lady-killer, from his tasselled French cap to his pointed patent leathers. Behind him walked a valet, carrying a brass-bound mahogany box, a clumsy easel, and a camp-stool.

"Going painting again, Ferdinand?" said his lordship, in a tone of some little scorn and irritation.

"Yes," said Ferdinand, rather idly, "I am going painting. Your man hasn't arrived yet?" He cast a glance of lazy amusement at the ladder and at the tools that lay at its feet.

"No," returned his lordship, irritably. "Worthless scoundrel. Ah! here he comes. Go away. Go away. Go and paint. Go and paint."

The young gentleman lifted his cap and sauntered on, turning once or twice to look at his lordship and a queer lop-sided figure shambling rapidly towards him.

"Joseph Beaker," said the Earl of Barfield, shaking his hand at the lop-sided man, "you are late again. I have been waiting ten minutes."

"What did I say yesterday?" asked Joseph Beaker. His face was lop-sided, like his figure, and his speech came in a hollow mumble which was difficult to follow. Joseph was content to pass as the harmless lunatic of the parish, but there was a shrewdly humorous twinkle in his eye which damaged his pretensions with the more discerning sort of people.

"I do not want to know what you said yesterday," his lordship answered, tartly. "Take up the billhook and the saw.

Now bring the ladder."

"What I said yesterday," mumbled Joseph, shambling by the nobleman's side, a little in the rear.

"Joseph Beaker," said the earl, "hold your tongue."

"Niver could do it," replied Joseph; "it slips from betwixt the thumb and finger like a eel. What I said yesterday was, 'Why doesn't thee set thy watch by the parish church?' Thee'st got Barfield time, I reckon, and Barfield's allays a wick and ten minutes afore other placen."

The aged nobleman twinkled and took snuff.

"Joseph," said his lordship, "I am going to make a new arrangement with you."

"Time you did," returned Joseph, pausing, ostensibly to shift the ladder from one shoulder to the other, but really to feign indifference.

"I find ninepence a day too much."

"I've allays said so," Joseph answered, shambling a little nearer. "A sinful sight too much. And half on it wasted o' them white garmints."

"I find myself a little in want of exercise," said his lordship. "I shall carry the ladder from the first tree to the second, and you will carry it from the second to the third; then I shall carry it again, and then *you* will carry it again. We shall go on in that way the whole afternoon, and shall continue in that way so long as I stay here."

Joseph laughed. It was in his laugh that he chiefly betrayed the shortcomings of character. His smile was dry and full of cunning, but his laugh was fatuous.

"Naturally," pursued the earl, "I shall not pay you full wages for a half-day's work." Joseph's face fell into a look of ludicrous consternation. "I shall be generous, however—I shall be generous. I shall give you sixpence. Sixpence a day, Joseph, and I shall do half the work myself."

"It ar'n't to be done, gaffer," said Joseph, resolutely stopping short, and setting up the ladder in the roadway.

The old nobleman turned to face him with pretended anger.

"You are impertinent, Joseph."

"It caw't be done, my lord," his assistant mumbled, thrusting his head through a space in the ladder.

"Times are hard, Joseph," returned his lordship.

There had been a discernible touch of banter in his voice and manner when he had rebuked Joseph a second or two before, but he was very serious now indeed.

"Times are hard; expenses must be cut down. I can't afford more. Sixpence a day is three shillings a week, and three shillings a week is one hundred and fifty-six shillings a year—seven pounds sixteen. That is interest at three per cent, on a sum of two hundred and fifty-nine pounds ten shillings. That is a great amount to lie waste. While I pay you sixpence a day I am practically two hundred and fifty-nine pounds ten shillings poorer than I should be if I kept the sixpence a day to myself. I might just as well not have the money—it is of no use to me."

"Gi'e it to me, then," suggested Joseph, with a feeble gleam.

"Sixpence a day," said his lordship, "is really a great waste of money."

"It's cruel hard o' me," returned Joseph, betraying a sudden inclination to whimper. "If I was a lord I'd be a lord, I would."

"Joseph! Joseph! Joseph!" cried his lordship, sharply.

"It's cruel hard," said Joseph, whimpering outright. "I'd be a man *or* a mouse, if I was thee."

"I shall be generous," said the aged nobleman, relenting. "I shall give you a suit of clothes. I shall give you a pair of trousers and a waistcoat—a laced waistcoat—and a coat."

Joseph laughed again, but clouded a moment later.

"Theer's them as pets the back to humble the belly, and theer's them as pets the belly to humble the back," he said, rubbing his bristly chin on a rung of the ladder as he spoke. "What soort o' comfort is theer in a laced wescut, if a man's got nothing to stretch it out with?"

"Well, well, Joseph," returned the earl, "sixpence a day is a great deal of money. In these hard times I can't afford more."

"What I look at," said Joseph, "is, it robs me of my bit o' bacon. If I was t'ask annybody in Heydon Hay, 'Is Lord Barfield the man to rob a poor chap of his bit o' bacon?' they'd say, 'No.' That's what they'd say. 'No,' they'd say; 'niver dream of a such-like thing as happening Joseph.'"

His lordship fidgeted and took snuff.

"What his lordship 'ud be a deal likelier to do," pursued Joseph, declaiming, in imitation of his supposed interlocutor, with his head through the ladder, and waving the billhook and the saw gently in either hand, "'ud be to say as a poor chap as wanted it might goo up to the Hall kitchen and have a bite—that's what annybody 'ud say in Hey don Hay as happened to be inquired of."

Joseph's glance dwelt lingeringly and wistfully on his lordship's face as he watched for the effect of his speech. The old earl took snuff with extreme deliberateness.

"Very well, Joseph," he said, after a pause, "we will arrange it in that way. Sixpence a day. And now and then—now and then, Joseph, you may go and ask Dewson for a little cold meat. There is a great deal of waste in the kitchen. It will make little difference—little difference."

Things being thus happily arranged, his lordship drew a slip of paper from his pocket and began to study it with much interest as he walked. He began to chuckle, and the fire of strategic triumph lit his aged eyes. The day's itinerary was planned upon that slip of paper, and Lord Barfield had so arranged it that Joseph should carry the ladder all the long distances, while he himself should carry it all the short ones. Joseph on his side was equally satisfied with the arrangement, so far as he knew it, and gave himself up to the sweet influences of fancy. He saw a glorified edition of himself, attired in my lord's cast-off garments, and engaged in the act of stretching out the laced waistcoat in the kitchen at the Hall. The prospect grew so glorious that he could not hold his own joy and gratulation. It welled over in a series of hollow chuckles, and his lordship twinkled dryly as he walked in front, and took snuff with a double gusto.

"We shall begin," said his lordship, "at Mother Duke's. That laburnum has been an eyesore this many a day. We must be resolute, Joseph. I shall expect you to guard the ladder, and not to let it go, even if she should venture to strike you."

"Her took me very sharp over the knuckles with the rollin'-pin last time, governor," said Joseph. "But her'll be no more trouble to thee now; her's gone away."

"Gone away! Mother Duke gone away?"

"Yes," mumbled Joseph, "her's gone away. There's a little old maid as lives theer now—has been theer a wick to-day."

"That's a pity—that's a pity," said his lordship. "I should have liked another skirmish with Mother Duke. At least, Joseph," he added, with the air of a man who finds consolation in disappointment, "we'll trim the laburnum this time. At all events, we'll make a fight for it, Joseph—we'll make a fight for it." Here he took the billhook and the saw from his assistant, and strode on, swinging one of the tools in each hand.

"Theer'll be no need for a fight," returned Joseph. "Her's no higher than sixpenn'orth o' soap after a hard day's washing."

"That's wrong reckoning, Joseph," said the earl; "wrong reckoning. The smaller they are the more terrible they may be."

"I niver fled afore a little un," said Joseph. "I could allays face a little un." He spoke with a retrospective tone. His lordship eyed him askance with a twinkle of rich enjoyment, and took snuff with infinite relish, as if he took Joseph's mental flavor with it and found it delightful. "Mother Duke could strike a sort of a fear into a man," pursued Joseph.

"What did you say was the new tenant's name, Joseph?" his lordship demanded, presently.

"Dunno," said Joseph. "Her's a little un—very straight up. Goes about on her heels like, to mek the most of herself."

A minute's further walk brought them to a bend in the lane, and, passing this, they paused before a cottage. The front of this cottage was overgrown with climbing roses, just then in full bloom, and a disorderly patch of overgrown blossom and shrub lay on each side the thread of gravel-walk which led from the gate to the door. A little personage, attired in a tight-fitting bodice and a girlish-looking skirt, was busily reducing the redundant growth to order with a pair of quick-snapping shears. It gave his lordship an odd kind of shock when this little personage arose and turned. The face was old. There was youth in the eyes and the delicate dark-brown arch of the eyebrows, but the old-fashioned ringlet which hung at either cheek beneath the cottage bonnet she wore was almost white. The cheeks were sunken from what had once been a charming contour, the delicate aquiline nose was pinched ever so little, the lips were dry, and there were fine wrinkles everywhere. There was something almost eerie in the youthfulness of the eyes, which shone in the midst of all her faded souvenirs of beauty. Had the eyes been old the face would have been beautiful still, but the contrast they presented to their setting was too striking for beauty. They gave the old face a curiously exalted look, an expression hardly indicative of complete sanity, though every feature was expressive in itself of keen good-sense, quick apprehension, and strong self-reliance.

The figure in its tight-fitting bodice looked like that of a girl of seventeen, but the stature was no more than that of a well-grown girl of twelve. The movement with which she had arisen and the attitude she took were full of life and vivacity.

David Christie Murray

His lordship was so taken aback by the extraordinary mixture of age and girlishness she presented that he stared for a second or two unlike a man of the world, and only recovered himself by an effort.

"Set up the ladder here, Joseph," he said, pointing with the billhook to indicate the place. Joseph set down the ladder on the pathway, and leaning it across the close-clipped privet hedge where numberless small staring eyes of white wood betrayed the recent presence of the shears, he propped it against the stout limb of a well-pruned apple-tree. His lordship, somewhat ostentatiously avoiding the eye of the inmate of the cottage, tucked his saw and his billhook under his left arm and mounted slowly, while Joseph made a great show of steadying the ladder. The little old woman opened the garden gate with a click and slipped into the roadway. His lordship hung his saw upon a rung of the ladder, and leaning a little over took a grasp of the bough of a sweeping laburnum which overhung the road.

"My lord," said a quick, thin voice, which in its blending of the characteristics of youth and age matched strangely with the speaker's aspect, "this tenement and its surrounding grounds are my freehold. I cannot permit your lordship to lay a mutilating hand upon them."

"God bless my soul!" said his lordship. "That's Rachel Blythe! That must be Rachel Blythe."

"Rachel Blythe at your lordship's service," said the little old lady. She dropped a curt little courtesy, at once as young and as old as everything about her, and stood looking up at him, with drooping hands crossed upon the garden shears.

"God bless my soul! Dear me!" said his lordship. "Dear me! God bless my soul!" He came slowly down the ladder and, surrendering his billhook to Joseph, advanced and proffered a tremulous white hand. Miss Blythe accepted it with a second curt little courtesy, shook it once up and down and dropped it. "Welcome back to Heydon Hay, Miss Blythe," said the old nobleman, with something of an air of gallantry. "You have long deprived us of your presence."

Perhaps Miss Blythe discerned a touch of badinage in his tone, and construed it as a mockery. She drew up her small figure in exaggerated dignity, and made much such a motion with her head and neck as a hen makes in walking.

"I have long been absent from Heydon Hay, my lord," she answered. "My good man," turning upon Joseph, "you may remove that ladder. His lordship can have no use for it here."

"Oh, come, come, Miss Blythe," said his lordship. "Manorial rights, manorial rights. This laburnum overhangs the road and prevents people of an average height from passing."

"If your lordship is aggrieved I must ask your lordship to secure a remedy in a legal manner."

"But really now. Observe, Miss Blythe, I can't walk under these boughs without knocking my hat off." He illustrated this statement by walking under the boughs. His cap fell on the dusty road, and Joseph, having picked it up, returned it to him.

"Your lordship is above the average height," said Miss Blythe— "considerably."

"No, no," the earl protested. "Not at all, not at all."

"I beg your lordship's pardon," said the little old lady, with stately politeness. "Nobody," she added, "who was not profoundly disloyal would venture to describe the Queen's Most Excellent Majesty as undersized. I am but a barleycorn less in stature than her Most Excellent Majesty, and your lordship is yards taller than myself."

"My dear Miss Blythe—" his lordship began, with hands raised in protest against this statement.

"Your lordship will pardon me," Miss Blythe interposed, swiftly, "if I say that at my age—forgive me if I say at your lordship's also—the language of conventional gallantry is unbecoming."

The little old lady said this with so starched and prim an air, and through this there peeped so obvious a satisfaction in rebuking him upon such a theme, that his lordship had to flourish his handkerchief from his pocket to hide his laughter.

"I have passed the last quarter of a century of my life," pursued Miss Blythe, "in an intimate if humble capacity in the service of a family of the loftiest nobility. I am not unacquainted with the airs and graces of the higher powers, but between your lordship and myself, at our respective ages, I cannot permit them to be introduced."

His lordship had a fit of coughing which lasted him two or three minutes, and brought the tears to his eyes. Most people might have thought that the cough bore a suspicious resemblance to laughter, but no such idea occurred to Miss Blythe.

"You are quite right, Miss Blythe," said the old nobleman, when he could trust himself to speak. He was twitching and twinkling with suppressed mirth, but he contained himself heroically. "I beg your pardon, and I promise that I will not again transgress in that manner. But really, that—that—fit of coughing has quite exhausted me for the moment. May I beg your permission to sit down?"

"Certainly, my lord," replied the little old lady, and in a bird-like fashion fluttered to the gate. It was not until she had reached the porch of the cottage that she became aware of the fact that the earl was following her. "Your lordship's pardon," she said then; "I will bring your lordship a chair into the garden. I am alone," she added, more prim and starched than ever, "and I have my reputation to consider."

Miss Blythe entered the cottage and returned with a chair, which she planted on the gravelled pathway. The old nobleman sat down and took snuff, twitching and twinkling in humorous enjoyment.

"How long is it since you left us?" he asked. "It looks as if it were only yesterday."

"I have been absent from Heydon Hay for more than a quarter of a century," the little old lady answered.

"Ah!" said he, and for a full minute sat staring before him rather forlornly. He recovered himself with a slight shake and resumed the talk. "You maintain your reputation for cruelty, Miss Blythe?"

"For cruelty, my lord?" returned Miss Blythe, with a transparent pretence of not understanding him.

"Breaking hearts," said his lordship, "eh? I was elderly before you went away, you know, but I remember a disturbance—a disturbance." He rapped with the knuckles of his left hand on his white kerseymere waistcoat. Miss Blythe tightened her lips and regarded him with an uncompromising air.

"Differences of sex, alone, my lord," she said, with decision, "should preclude a continuance of this conversation."

"Should they?" asked the old nobleman. "Do you really think so? I forget. I am a monument of old age, and I forget, but I fancy I used to think otherwise. You were the beauty of the place, you know. Is that a forbidden topic also?"

Miss Blythe blushed ever so little, but her curiously youthful eyes smiled, and it was plain she was not greatly displeased. The Earl of Barfield went quiet again, and again stared straight before him with a somewhat forlorn expression. The little old lady reminded him of her mother, and the remembrance of her mother reminded him of his own youth. He woke up suddenly. "So you've come back?" he said, abruptly. "You've bought the cottage?"

"The freehold of the cottage was purchased for me by my dear mistress," said the little old lady. "I desired to end my days where I began them."

"H'm!" said my lord. "We're going to be neighbors? We *are* neighbors. We must dwell together in unity. Miss Blythe— we must dwell together in unity. I have my hands pretty full this afternoon, and I must go. I'll just trim these laburnums, and alter—"

"I beg your lordship's pardon," said Miss Blythe, with decision, "your lordship will do nothing of the sort."

"Eh? Oh, nonsense, nonsense! Must clear the footway. Must have the footway clear—really must. Besides, it improves the aspect of the garden. Always does. Decidedly improves it. Joseph Beaker, hold the ladder."

Talking thus, the old gentleman had arisen from his chair and had re-entered the roadway, but the little old lady skimmed past him and faced him at the foot of the ladder.

"If your lordship wants to cut trees," she said, "your lordship may cut your lordship's own."

"Up thee goest, gaffer," said Joseph, handing over the little old lady's head the billhook and the saw.

Miss Blythe turned upon him with terrible majesty.

"Joseph Beaker?" she said, regarding him inquiringly. "Ah! The passage of six-and-twenty years has not improved your intellectual condition. Take up that ladder, Joseph Beaker. If you should ever dare again to place it against a tree upon my freehold property I shall call the policeman. I will set man-traps," pursued the little old lady, shaking her curls vigorously at Joseph. "I will have spring-guns placed in the trees."

"Her's wuss than t'other un," mumbled the routed Joseph, as he shambled in his lop-sided fashion down the road. "I should ha' thought you could ha' done what you liked wi' a little un like that. I niver counted on being forced to flee afore a little un."

The earl said nothing, and Miss Blythe, satisfied that the retreat was real, had already gone back to her gardening.

CHAPTER III

In the mean time the young man in the tasselled cap and the patent-leathers had strolled leisurely in the opposite direction to that the earl had taken, and in a little while—still followed by the valet, who bore his painting tools—had climbed into a field knee-deep in grass which was ready for the scythe. At the bottom of this meadow ran a little purling stream, with a slant willow growing over it. In obedience to the young gentleman's instructions, the valet set down his burden here, and having received orders to return in an hour's time, departed. The young gentleman sketched the willow and the brook in no very masterly fashion, but at a sort of hasty random, and tiring of his self-imposed task before half an hour was over, threw himself at length beside the brook, and there, lulled by the ripple of the water and the slumberous noise of insects, fell asleep. The valet's returning footsteps awoke him. He rolled over idly and lit a new cigar.

"Shall I take back the things to the Hall, sir?" asked the servant.

"Yes, take them back to the Hall," said the young gentleman, lazily. Rising to his feet, he produced a small pocket-mirror, and having surveyed the reflection of his features, arranged his scarf, cocked his cap, and sauntered from the field. His way led him past a high time-crumbled wall, over which a half score of trees pushed luxuriant branches. The wall was some ten feet in height, and in the middle of it was a green-painted door which opened inward. It was not quite closed, and a mere streak of sunlit grass could be seen within.

As the idle young gentleman sauntered along with his hands folded behind him, his eyes half closed, and his nose in the air, a sudden burst of music reached his ears and brought him to a stand-still. It surprised him a little, partly because it was extremely well played, and partly because the theme was classic and but little known. He moved his head from side to side to make out, if possible, the inmates of the garden, but he could see nothing but the figure of a girl, who leaned her hands upon a tree and her cheek upon her hands. This, however, was enough to pique curiosity, for the figure was singularly graceful, and had fallen into an attitude of unstudied elegance. He pushed the door an inch wider, and so far enlarged his view that he could see the musicians—three old men and a young one—who sat in the middle of a grassy space and ploughed away at the music with a will. Not caring to be observed in his clandestine espial he drew back a little, still keeping the figure of the girl in sight, and listened to the music.

He was so absorbed that the sudden spectacle of the Earl of Barfield, who came round the corner with a ladder on his shoulder, startled him a little. His lordship was followed by Joseph Beaker, who bore the saw and the billhook, and the old nobleman was evidently somewhat fatigued, and carried the ladder with difficulty. Seeing his young friend, he propped his burden against the wall and mopped his forehead, casting an upward glance at the boughs which stretched their pleasant shadow overhead.

"Well, Ferdinand," he said, in a discontented voice, "what are you doing here?"

"I am listening to the music," said Ferdinand, in answer.

"The music?" said his lordship. "That caterwauling?" He waved a hand towards the wall. "Old Fuller and his friends."

"They play capitally," said Ferdinand; "for country people they play capitally. They are amateurs, of course?"

"Do they?" asked the earl, somewhat eagerly; "do they, really? Tell 'em so, tell 'em so. Nothing so likely"—he dropped his voice to a whisper—"nothing so likely to catch old Fuller's vote as that. He's mad on music. I haven't ventured to call on him for a long time. We had quite a little fracas years ago about these overhanging boughs. They're quite an eyesore—quite an eyesore; but he won't have 'em touched; won't endure it. Joseph, you can carry the ladder home. We'll go in, Ferdinand—it's an admirable opportunity. I've been wondering how to approach old Fuller, and this is the very thing— the very thing."

"Wait until they have finished," said the younger man; and Joseph having shouldered the ladder and gone off with it in his own crab-like way, the two stood together until the musicians in the garden had finished the theme upon which they were engaged.

The earl pushed open the garden door and entered, Ferdinand following in the rear. The girl turned at the noise made by the shrieking hinges, and stood somewhat irresolutely, as if uncertain. Finally, she bowed in a manner sufficiently distant and ceremonious. Ferdinand put up an eye-glass and surveyed her with an air of criticism, while the old nobleman advanced briskly towards the table around which the musicians were seated.

"Good-day, Fuller, good-day," he said, in a hearty voice;

"don't let me disturb you, I beg. We heard your beautiful music as we passed by, and stopped to listen to it. This is my young friend, Mr. De Blacquaire, who's going to stand, you know, for this division of the county. Mr. De Blacquaire is a great amateur of music, and was delighted with your playing —delighted."

"I was charmed, indeed," said Ferdinand. "There are lovers of music everywhere, of course, but I had not expected to find so advanced a company of amateurs in Heydon Hay. That final passage was exquisitely rendered."

The earl stood with a smile distorted in the sunlight, looking alternately from the candidate to the voters.

"Exquisitely rendered, I am sure," he said—"exquisitely rendered. Praise from Mr. De Blacquaire is worth having, let me tell you, Fuller. Mr. De Blacquaire is himself a distinguished musician. Ah! my old friend Eld! How do you do? how do you do?"

This greeting was addressed to Sennacherib, who had arisen on the earl's arrival, had deliberately turned his back, and was now engaged in turning over the leaves of music which lay on the table before him.

"Sennacherib," said Isaiah, mildly, "his lordship's a-talking to thee."

"I can hear," responded Sennacherib, "as he's a-talking to one on us. As for me, I'm none the better for being axed."

"And none the worse, I hope," said his lordship, as cheerily as he could.

"Nayther wuss nor better, so far as I can see,"

replied Sennacherib.

"Come, come, Mr. Eld," said Fuller. "Harmony! harmony!"

"I was a-tekin' my walks abroad this mornin'," said Sennacherib, still bending over his music, "when I see that petted hound of the vicar's mek a fly at a mongrel dog as had a bone. The mongrel run for it and took the bone along with him. It comes into my mind now as if the hound had known a month or two aforehand as he'd want that bone, he'd ha' made friends wi' the mongrel."

This parable was so obviously directed at his lordship and his young *protege* that Sennacherib's companions looked and felt ill at ease. Fuller was heard to murmur "Harmony!" but a disconcerted silence fell on all, and his lordship took snuff while he searched for a speech which should turn the current of conversation into a pleasanter channel. The Earl of Barfield was particularly keen in his desire to run Mr. Ferdinand de Blacquaire for the county, and to run him into Parliament. Ferdinand himself was much less keen about the business, and regarded it all as a mingled joke and bore. This being the case, he felt free to avoid the ordinary allures of the parliamentary candidate, and, apart from that, he had, with himself at least, a reputation to sustain as a man of wit.

"Has this mongrel a bone?" he asked, in a silky tone. "Let him keep it."

His lordship shot a glance of surprised wrath at him, almost of horror, but Sennacherib began to chuckle.

"Pup's got a bite in him," said Sennacherib—"got a bite in him."

His lordship felt a little easier, and looking about him

discovered that everybody was smiling more or less, though on one or two faces the smile sat uneasily.

"Come, come, Mr. Eld," said Fuller, "harmony!"

"Ah!" cried the earl, seizing gladly on the word. "Let us have a little harmony. Don't let our presence disturb your music. Mr. Eld is a local notability, Ferdinand. Mr. Eld speaks his mind to everybody. I'm afraid he's on the other side, and in that case you'll have many a tussle with him before you come to the hustings. Eh? That's so, isn't it, Eld? Eh? That's so?"

"Oh," said Sennacherib, with the slow local drawl, "we'll tek a bit of a wrastle now and again, I mek no manner of a doubt."

"And in the mean time," said his lordship, "let us start harmoniously. Give us a little music, Fuller. Go on just as if we were not here."

"Ruth, my wench," said Fuller, "fetch his lordship a chair, and bring another for Mr.—" He hung upon the Mr., searching to recall the name.

"Devil-a-care," suggested Sennacherib.

"De Blacquaire," said the earl, correcting him. "Mr. Ferdinand de Blacquaire."

The girl had already moved away, and Ferdinand, with an air in which criticism melted slowly into approval, watched her through his eye-glass. The only young man in the quartette party, Reuben Gold, eyed Ferdinand with a look in which criticism hardened into disapproval, and, turning away, fluttered the edges of the music sheets before him with the tip of his bow.

David Christie Murray

"Look here, lads," said Fuller, "we'll have a slap at that there sonata of B. Thoven's, eh?"

"Beethoven?" asked Ferdinand, with a little unnecessary stress upon the name to mark his pronunciation of it. "You play Beethoven? This is extremely interesting." He spoke to the earl, who rubbed his hands and nodded. The young first-violin tossed his chestnut-colored mane on one side with a gesture of irritation. Ruth reappeared with a chair in each hand. They were old-fashioned and rather heavy, being built of solid oak, but she carried them lightly and gracefully. Ferdinand started forward and attempted to relieve her of her burden. At first she resisted, but he insisting upon the point she yielded. The young Ferdinand was less graceful than he had meant to be in the carriage of the chairs, and Ruth looked at Reuben with a smile so faint as scarcely to be perceptible. Reuben with knitted brows pored over his music, and the girl returned to her old place and her old attitude by the apple-tree.

Ferdinand, having the placing of the chairs in his own hands, took up a position in which, without being obtrusively near, he was close enough to address Ruth if occasion should arise, as he was already fairly resolved it should. The three elders were most drolly provincial, to his mind, and their accent was positively barbarous to his ears. Reuben was less provincial to look at, but to Mr. De Blacquaire's critical eye the young man was evidently not a gentleman. He had not heard him speak as yet, but could well afford to make up his mind without that. Nobody but a boof could have employed Reuben's tailor or his shoemaker. As for the girl, she looked like a lily in a kitchen-garden, a flower among the coarse and commonplace things of every-day consumption. It would be a deadly pity, he thought, if she should have an accent like the rest. Her dress was perfectly refined and simple, and Ferdinand guessed pretty shrewdly that this was likely to be due to her own handiwork and fancy.

"What a delightful, quaint old garden you have here, to be sure," he said.

With a perfect naturalness she raised a warning palm against him, and at that instant the quartette party began their performance. She had not even turned an eye in his direction, and he was a little piqued. The hand which had motioned him to silence was laid now on the gnarled old apple-tree, and she rested her ripe cheek against it. Her eyes began to dream at the music, and it was evident that her forgetfulness of the picturesque young gentleman beside her was complete and unaffected. The picturesque young gentleman felt this rather keenly. The snub was small enough, in all conscience, but it *was* a snub, and he was sensitive, even curiously sensitive, to that kind of thing. And he was not in the habit of being snubbed. He was accustomed to look for the signs of his own power to please among young women who moved in another sphere.

It was a very, very small affair, but then it is precisely these very small affairs which rankle in a certain sort of mind. Ferdinand dismissed it, but it spoiled his music for the first five minutes.

The Earl of Barfield was one of those people to whom music is neither more nor less than noise. He loved quiet and hated noise, and the four interpreters of the melody and harmony of Beethoven afforded him as much delight as so many crying children would have done. It had been a joke against him in his youth that he had once failed to distinguish between "God save the King" and the "Old Hundredth." Harmony and melody here were alike divine in themselves, and were more than respectably rendered, and he sat and suffered under them in his young friend's behoof like a hero.

They bored him unspeakably, and the performance lasted half an hour. When it was all over he beat his withered white hands together once or twice, and smiled in self-gratulation that his time of suffering was over.

"Admirably rendered!" cried Ferdinand; "admirably—admirably rendered. Will you forgive me just a hint, sir?" He addressed Sennacherib. "A leetle more light and shade! A performance less level in tone."

"P'raps the young man'll show us how to do it," said Sennacherib, in a dry, mock humility, handing his fiddle and bow towards the critic.

The critic accepted them with a manner charmingly unconscious of the intended satire, and walked round the table until he came behind Reuben, when he turned back the music for a leaf or two.

"Here, for example," he said, and tucking the instrument beneath his chin, played through a score of bars with a certain exaggerated *chic* which awakened Sennacherib's derision.

"What dost want to writhe i' that fashion for?" he demanded. "Dost find thine inwards twisted? It's a pretty tone, though," he allowed. "The young man can fiddle. Strikes me, young master, as thee'dst do better at the Hopera than the House o' Commons. Tek a fool's advice and try."

Ferdinand smiled with genuine good-humor. This insolent old personage began to amuse him.

"Really I don't know, sir," he answered. "Perhaps I may do pretty well in the House of Commons, if you will be good enough to try me. One can't please everybody, but I promise to do my best."

"The best can do no more," said Fuller, in a mellow, peace-making kind of murmur; "the best can do no more."

"I've no mind for that theer whisperin' and shout-in' in the course of a piece of music," said Sennacherib. "Pianner is pianner, and forte is forte, but theer's no call to strain a man's ears to listen to the one, nor to drive him deaf with t'other. Same time, if the young gentleman 'ud like to come an' gi'e us a lesson now and then we'd tek it."

"I'm not able to give you lessons, sir," returned Mr. De Blacquaire, with unshaken good-humor; "but if you'll allow me to take one now and then by listening, I shall be delighted."

"Nothin' agen that, is theer, Mr. Fuller?" demanded Sennacherib.

"Allays pleased to see the young gentleman," responded Fuller.

"When may I come to listen to you again, gentlemen?" asked Ferdinand. His manner was full of *bonhomie* now, and had no trace of affectation. It pleased everybody but Reuben, who had conceived a distaste for him from the first. Perhaps, if he had not placed his chair so near to Ruth, and had regarded her less often and with a less evident admiration, the young man might have liked him better.

"Well," said Fuller, "we are here pretty nigh every evenin' while the fine weather lasts. We happen to be here this afternoon because young Mr. Gold is goin' away for to-night to Castle Barfield. You'll find we here almost of any evenin'—to-morrow, to begin with."

"We had better be going now, Ferdinand," said his lordship, who dreaded the new beginning of the music. "Good-afternoon, Fuller. Good-afternoon, Eld. Good-afternoon, Gold."

"Good-day, my lord," said Reuben, rather gloomily. He had not spoken until now, and Ferdinand had wished to note the accent. There was none to note in the few words he uttered.

"Your little girl is growing into a woman, Fuller," said his lordship.

"That's the way wi' most gells, my lord," said Fuller.

"Good-afternoon, Miss Ruth," said the old nobleman, nodding and smiling.

"Good-afternoon, my lord," said Ruth. Ferdinand's attentive ear noted again the absence of the district accent. He removed his cap and bowed to her.

"Good-afternoon. I may come to-morrow evening, then?" The query was addressed to her, but she did not answer it, either by glance or word. She had answered his bow and turned away before he had spoken.

"Ay," said Fuller; "come and welcome."

He bowed and smiled all round, and walked away with his lordship. He turned at the garden door for a final glance at the pretty girl, but she had her back turned upon him, and was leaning both hands on her father's shoulder.

CHAPTER IV

The rustic little church at Heydon Hay made a nucleus for the village, which, close at hand, clustered about it pretty thickly, but soon began to fray off into scattered edges, as if the force of attraction decreased with distance, after the established rule. Beside the church-yard, and separated from it by a high brick wall, was a garden, fronted by half a dozen slim and lofty poplars. Within the churchyard the wall was only on a level with the topmost tufts of grass, but on the garden side it stood six feet high, and was bulged out somewhat by the weight of earth which pressed against it. Facing the tall poplars was a house of two stories. It looked like a short row of houses, for it boasted three front doors. Over each of these was hung a little contrivance which resembled a section of that extinguisher apparatus which is still to be found suspended above the pulpit in some old-fashioned country churches. All the windows of the old house were of diamond panes, and those of the upper story projected from the roof of solid and venerable thatch. A pair of doves had their home in a wicker cage which hung from the wall, and their cooing was like the voice of the house, so peaceful, homely, and Old-world was its aspect.

Despite the three front doors, the real entrance to the house was at the rear, to which access was had by a side gate. A path, moss-grown at the edges, led between shrubs and flowers to a small circle of brickwork, in the midst of which was a well with rope and windlass above it, and thence continued to the door, which led to an antique, low-browed kitchen. A small dark passage led from the kitchen to a front room with a great fireplace, which rose so high that there was but just enough room between the mantle-board and the whitewashed ceiling for the squat brass candlesticks and the big foreign sea-shells which stood there for ornament.

The diamonded window admitted so little light that on entering here from the outer sunshine the visitor could only make out the details one by one. When his eyes became accustomed to the semi-darkness he was sure to notice a dozen or more green baize bags which hung upon the walls, each half defining, in the same vague way as all the others, the outline of the object it contained. Each green baize bag was closely tied at the neck, and suspended at an equal height with the rest upon a nail. There was something of a vault-like odor in the room, traceable probably to the two facts that the carpet was laid upon a brick floor, and that the chamber was rarely opened to the air.

Ezra Gold, seated upright in an oaken arm-chair, with a hand lightly grasping the end of either arm, was at home in the close, cool shadow of the place. The cloistered air, the quiet and the dim shade seemed to suit him, and he to be in harmony with them. His eyes were open, and alighted now and again with an air of recognition on some familiar object, but otherwise he might have seemed asleep. On the central table was a great pile of music-books, old-fashioned alike in shape and binding. They exhaled a special cloistral odor of their own, as if they had been long imprisoned. Ezra's eye dwelt oftener on these musty old books than elsewhere.

He had sat still and silent for a long time, when the bells of the church, with a startling nearness and distinctness, broke into a peal. He made a slight movement when the sound first fell upon his ear, but went back to his quiet and his dreams again at once.

Ten minutes went by and the bells were still pealing, when he heard a sound which would have been inaudible in the midst of the metallic clamor to ears less accustomed than his own. He had lived there all his life, and scarcely noticed the noise which would almost have deafened a stranger. The sound he had heard was the clicking of the gate, and after a pause it was followed by the appearance of his nephew Reuben, who looked about him with a dazzled and uncertain gaze.

"Well, Reuben, lad?" said the old man; but his voice was lost for his nephew in the noise which shook the air. "Dost not see me?" he cried, speaking loudly this time.

"I'm fresh from the sunlight," Reuben shouted, with unnecessary force. "You spoke before. I couldn't hear you for the bells."

The old man with a half-humorous gesture put his hands to his ears.

"No need to shout a man's head off," he answered. "Come outside."

Rueben understood the gesture, though he could not hear the words, and the two left the room together, and came out upon the back garden. The sound of the bells was still clear and loud, but by no means so overwhelming as it had been within-doors.

"That's better," said Reuben. "They're making noise enough for young Sennacherib's wedding."

"Young Sennacherib?" asked his uncle. "Young Eld? Is young Eld to be married?"

"Didn't you Know that? The procession is coming along the road this minute. Old Sennacherib disapproves of the match, and we've had a scene the like of which was never known in Heydon Hay before."

"Ay?" said Ezra, with grave interest, slowly, and with a look of a man long imprisoned, to whom outside things are strange, but interesting still. "As how?"

"Why thus," returned Reuben, with a laugh in his eyes. "Old Sennacherib comes to his gate and awaits the wedding-party. Young Snac, with his bride upon his arm, waves a braggart handkerchief at the oldster, and out walks papa, plants himself straight in front of the company, and brings all to a halt. 'I should like to tell thee,' says the old fellow before them all, rolling that bull-dog head of his, 'as I've made my will an' cut thee off with a shillin'!'"

"Dear me!" said Ezra, seriously; "dear me! And what answer made young Snac to this?"

"Young Snac," said Reuben, "was equal to his day. 'All right,' says he; 'gi'e me the shillin' now, an' we'll drop in at the "Goat" and split a quart together.' 'All right,' says the old bull-dog; 'it's th' on'y chance I shall ever light upon of mekin' a profit out o' thee.' He lugs out a leather bag, finds a shilling, bites it to make sure of its value, hands it to the young bull-dog, and at the 'Goat' they actually pull up together, and young Snac spends the money then and there. 'Bring out six pints,' cries Snac the younger. 'Fo'penny ale's as much as a father can expect when his loving son is a-spendin' the whole of his inheritance upon him.' Everybody sipped, the bride included, and the two bull-dogs clinked their mugs together. I sipped myself, being invited as a bystander, and toasted father and son together."

"But, mind thee, lad," said Ezra, "it's scarcely to be touched upon as a laughing matter. Drollery of a sort theer is in it, to be sure; but what Sennacherib Eld says he sticks to. When he bites he holds. He was ever of that nature."

"I know," said Reuben; "but young Nip-and-Fasten has the breed of old Bite-and-Hold-Fast in him, and if the old man keeps his money the young one will manage to get along without it."

At this moment the bells ceased their clangor.

"They've gone into the church, Reuben," said the old man. "I'll do no less than wish 'em happiness, though there's fewer that finds it than seeks it by that gate."

"It's like other gates in that respect, I suppose," Reuben answered.

"Well, yes," returned the elder man, lingeringly. "But it's the gate that most of 'em fancy, and thereby it grows the saddest to look at, lad. Come indoors again. There'll be no more bells this yet-awhile."

Reuben followed him into the cloistral odors and shadows of the sitting-room. Ezra took his old seat, and kept silence for the space of two or three minutes.

"You said you wanted to speak to me, uncle," said the younger man, at length.

"Yes, yes," said Ezra, rising as if from a dream. "You're getting to have a very pretty hand on the fiddle, Reuben, and—well, it's a shame to bury anything that has a value. This"—he arose and laid a hand on the topmost book of the great pile of music—"this has never seen the light for a good five-and-twenty year. Theer's some of it forgot, notwithstanding that it's all main good music. But theer's no room i' the world for th' old-fangled an' the newfangled. One nail drives out another. But I've been thinking thee mightst find a thing or two herein as would prove of value, and it's yours if you see fit to take it away."

"Why, it's a library," said Reuben. "You are very good, uncle, but—"

"Tek it, lad, tek it, if you'd like it, and make no words. And if it shouldn't turn out to have been worth the carrying you can let th' old chap think it was—eh?"

"Worth the carrying?" said Reuben, with a half-embarrassed little laugh. "I'm pretty sure you had no rubbish on your shelves, uncle." He began to turn over the leaves of the topmost book. "'*Etudes?*" he read, "'*pour deux violins, par* Joseph Manzini.' This looks good. Who was Joseph Manzini? I never heard of him."

"Manzini?" asked the old man, with a curious eagerness— "Manzini." His voice changed altogether, and fell into a dreamy and retrospective tone. He laid a hand upon the open pages, and smoothed them with a touch which looked like a caress.

"Who was he?" asked Reuben. "Did you know him?"

"No, lad," returned the old man, coming out of his dream, and smiling as he spoke, "I never knew him. What should bring me to know a German musician as was great in his own day?"

"I thought you spoke as if you knew him," said Reuben.

"Hast a quick ear," said Ezra, "and a searching fancy. No, lad, no; I never knew him. But that was the last man I ever handled bow and fiddle for. I left that open" (he tapped the book with his fingers and then closed it as he spoke)—"I left that open on my table when I was called away on business to London. I found it open when I came home again, and I closed it, for I never touched a bow again. I'd heard Paganini in the mean time. Me and 'Saiah Eld tried that through together, and since then I've never drawn a note out o' catgut."

"I could never altogether understand it, uncle," said Reuben. "What could the man's playing have been like?"

"What was it like?" returned the older man. "What is theer as it wa'n't like? I couldn't tell thee, lad—I couldn't tell thee. It was like a lost soul a-wailing i' the pit. It was like an angel a-sing-ing afore the Lord. It was like that passage i' the Book o' Job, where 'tis said as 'twas the dead o' night when deep sleep falleth upon men, and a vision passed afore his face, and the hair of his flesh stood up. It was like the winter tempest i' the trees, and a little brook in summer weather. It was like as if theer was a livin' soul within the thing, and sometimes he'd trick it and soothe it, and it'd laugh and sing to do the heart good, an' another time he'd tear it by the roots till it chilled your blood."

"You heard him often?" asked Reuben.

"Never but once," said Ezra, shaking his head with great decision. "Never but once. He wa'n't a man to hear too often. 'Twas a thing to know and to carry away. A glory to have looked at once, but not to live in the midst on. Too bright for common eyes, lad—too bright for common eyes."

"I've heard many speak of his playing," said Reuben. "But there are just as many opinions as there are people."

"There's no disputing in these matters," the older man answered. "I've heard him talked of as a Charley Tann, which I tek to be a kind of humbugging pretender, but 'twas plain to see for a man with a soul behind his wescut as the man was wore to a shadow with his feeling for his music. 'Twas partly the man's own sufferin' and triumphin' as had such a power over me. It is with music as th' other passions. % Theer's love, for example. A lad picks out a wench, and spends his heart and natur' in her behalf as free as if there'd niver been a wench i' the world afore, and niver again would be. And after all a wench is a commonish sort of a object, and even the wench the lad's in love with is a commonish sort o' creature among wenches. But what's that to him, if her chances to be just the sort his soul and body cries after?"

"Ah!" said Reuben, "*if* his soul cries after her. But if he values goodness his soul will cry after it, and if he values beauty his soul will cry after that. I never heard Paganini, but he was a great player, or a real lover of music like you would never have found what he wanted in him."

"Yes, lad," his uncle answered, falling suddenly into his habitual manner, "the man was a player. Thee canst have the music any time thee likst to send for it."

Reuben knew the old man and his ways. The talkative fit was evidently over, and he might sit and talk, if he would, from then till evening, and get no more than a monosyllable here and there in return for his pains.

"It will take a hand-cart to carry the books," he said; "but I will take Manzini now if you will let me." The old man, contenting himself with a mere nod in answer, he took up the old-fashioned oblong folio, tucked it under his arm, and shook hands with the donor. "This is a princely gift, uncle," he said, with the natural exaggeration of a grateful youngster. "I don't know how to say thank you for it."

Ezra smiled, but said nothing. Reuben, repeating his leave-taking, went away, and coming suddenly upon the bright sunlight and the renewed clangor of the bells, was half stunned by the noise and dazzled by the glare. With all this clash and brilliance, as if they existed because of her, and were a part of her presence, appeared Ruth Fuller in the act of passing Ezra's house. Ruth had brightness, but it was rather of the twilight sort than this; and the music which seemed fittest to salute her apparition might have been better supplied by these same bells at a distance of a mile or two. Reuben was perturbed, as any mere mortal might expect to be on encountering a goddess.

Let us see the goddess as well as may be.

She was country-bred to begin with, and though to Heydon Hay her appearance smacked somewhat of the town, a dweller in towns would have called her rustic. She wore a straw hat which was in the fashion of the time, and to the eyes of the time looked charming, though twenty years later we call it ugly, and speak no more than truth. Beneath this straw hat very beautiful and plenteous brown hair escaped in defiance of authority, and frolicked into curls and wavelets, disporting itself on a forehead of creamy tone and smoothness, and just touching the eyebrows, which were of a slightly darker brown, faintly arched on the lower outline, and more prominently arched on the upper. Below the brows brown eyes, as honest as the day, and with a frank smile always ready to break through the dream which pretty often filled them. A short upper lip, delicately curved and curiously mobile, a full lower lip, a chin expressive of great firmness, but softened by a dimpled hollow in the very middle of its roundness, a nose neither Grecian nor tilted, but betwixt the two, and delightful, and a complexion familiar with sun and air, wholesome, robust, and fine. In stature she was no more than on a level with Reuben's chin; but Reuben was taller than common, standing six feet in his stockings. This fact of superior height was not in itself sufficient to account for the graceful inclination of the body which always characterized Reuben when he talked with Ruth. There was a tender and unconscious deference in his attitude which told more to the least observant observer than Reuben would willingly have had known.

Ezra Gold saw the chance encounter through the window, and watched the pair as they shook hands. They walked away together, for they were bound in the same direction, and the old man rose from his seat and walked to the window to look after them.

"Well, well, lad," he said, speaking half aloud, after the fashion of men who spend much of their time alone, "theert beauty and goodness theer, I fancy. Go thy ways, lad, and be happy."

They were out of sight already, and Ezra, with his hands folded behind him, paced twice or thrice along the room. Pausing before one of the green baize bags, he lifted it from its nail, and having untied the string that fastened it, he drew forth with great tenderness an unstrung violin, and, carrying it to the light, sat down and turned it over and over in his hands. Then he took the neck with his left hand, and, placing the instrument upright upon his knee, caressed it with his right.

"Poor lass," he said, "a' might think as thee was grieved to have had ne'er a soul to sing to all these years. I've a half mind to let thee have a song now, but I doubt thee couldst do naught but screech at me. I've forgotten how to ask a lady of thy make to sing. Shalt go to Reuben, lass; he'll mek thee find thy voice again. Rare and sweet it used to be—rare and sweet."

He fell into a fit of coughing which shook him from head to foot, but even in the midst of the paroxysm he made shift to lay down the violin with perfect tenderness. When the fit was over he lay back in his chair with his arms depending feebly at his sides, panting a little, but smiling like a man at peace.

CHAPTER V

These had been a long spell of fair weather, and the Earl of Barfield had carried on his warfare against all and sundry who permitted the boughs of their garden trees to overhang the public highway, for a space of little less than a month. The campaign had been conducted with varying success, but the old nobleman counted as many victories as fights, and was disposed, on the whole, to be content with himself. He was an old and experienced warrior in this cause, and had learned to look with a philosophic eye upon reverses.

But on the day following that which saw the introduction of his lordship's parliamentary nominee to the quartette party, his lordship encountered a check which called for all the resources of philosophy. He was routed by his own henchman, Joseph Beaker.

The defeat arrived in this wise: his lordship having carefully arranged his rounds so that Joseph should carry the ladder all the long distances while he himself bore it all the short ones, had found himself so flurried by the defeat he had encountered at the hands of Miss Blythe, that he had permitted Joseph to take up the ladder and carry it away from where it had leaned against the apple-tree in the little old lady's garden. This unforeseen incident had utterly disarranged his plans, and since he had been unadvised enough to post his servitor in the particulars of the campaign, Joseph had been quick to discover his own advantage.

"We will go straight on to Willis's, Joseph," said his lordship, when they began their rounds that afternoon. The stroke was simple, but, if it should only succeed, was effective.

"We bain't a-goin' to pass Widder Hotchkiss, be we, governor?" demanded Joseph, who saw through the device. His lordship decided not to hear the question, and walked on a little ahead, swinging the billhook and the saw.

Joseph Beaker revolved in his mind his own plan of action. In front of Widow Hotchkiss's cottage the trees were unusually luxuriant, and the boughs hung unusually low. When they were reached, Joseph contrived to entangle his ladder and to bring himself to a stand-still, with every appearance of naturalness.

"My blessed!" he mumbled, "this here's a disgrace to the parish, gaffer. Theer's nothin' in all Heydon Hay as can put a patch on it. Thee bissent agoin' past this, beest? Her's as small-sperited as a rabbit—the widder is."

"We'll take it another time, Joseph," said his lordship, striving to cover his confusion by taking a bigger pinch of snuff than common—"another time, Joseph, another time."

"Well," said Joseph, tossing his lop-sided head, as if he had at last fathomed the folly and weakness of human nature, and resigned himself to his own mournful discoveries, "I should niver ha' thought it." He made a show of shouldering the ladder disgustedly, but dropped it again. "We fled afore a little un yesterday," he said. "I did look for a show o' courage here, governor." His lordship hesitated. "Why, look at it," pursued Joseph, waving a hand towards the overhanging

David Christie Murray

verdure; "it 'ud be a sinful crime to go by it."

"Put up the ladder, Joseph," replied his lordship, in a voice of sudden resolve. The Hotchkiss case was a foregone victory for him, and his own desires chimed with Joseph's arguments, even while he felt himself outgeneralled.

The widow sweetened the business by a feeble protest, and the Earl of Barfield was lordly with ner.

"Must come down, my good woman," said his lordship, firmly, "must come down. Obstruct the highway. Disgrace to the parish."

"That's what I said," mumbled Joseph, as he steadied the ladder from below. The widow watched the process wistfully, and my lord chopped and sawed with unwonted gusto. Branch after branch fell into the lane, and the aged nobleman puffed and sweated with his grateful labor. He had not had such a joyful turn for many a day. The widow moaned like a winter wind in a key-hole, and when his lordship at last descended from his perch she was wiping her eyes with her apron.

"I know full well what poor folks has got to put up with at the hands o' them as the Lord has set in authority," said the widow, "but it's cruel hard to have a body's bits o' trees chopped and lopped i' that way. When ourn was alive his lordship niver laid a hand upon 'em. Ourn 'ud niver ha' bent himself to put up wi' it, that he niver would, and Lord Barfield knows it; for though he was no better nor a market-gardener, he was one o' them as knowed what was becomin' between man and man, be he niver so lowly, and his lordship the lord o' the manor for miles around."

"Tut, tut, my good woman," returned his lordship. "Pooh,

pooh! Do for firewood. Nice and dry against the winter. Much better there than obstructing the high-road—much better. Joseph Beaker, take the ladder."

"My turn next time," replied Joseph. "Carried it here."

His lordship, a little abashed, feigned to consider, and took snuff.

"Quite right, Joseph," he answered, "quite right. Quite fair to remind me. Perfectly fair." But he was a good deal blown and wearied with his exertions, and though anxious to escape the moanings of the widow he had no taste for the exercise which awaited him. He braced himself for the task, however, and handing the tools to his henchman, manfully shouldered the ladder and started away with it. The lane was circuitous, and when once he had rounded the first corner he paused and set down his burden. "It's unusually warm to-day, Joseph," he said, mopping at his wrinkled forehead.

"Theer's a coolish breeze," replied Joseph, "and a-plenty o' shadder."

"Do you know, Joseph," said the earl, in a casual tone, "I think I shall have to get you to take this turn. I am a little tired."

"Carried it last turn," said Joseph, decidedly. "A bargain's a bargain."

"Certainly, certainly," returned his lordship, "a bargain *is* a bargain, Joseph." He sat down upon one of the lower rungs of the ladder and fanned himself with a pocket-handkerchief. "But you know, Joseph," he began again after a pause, "nobody pushes a bargain too hard. If you carry the ladder this time I will carry it next. Come now—what do you say to that?"

"It's a quarter of a mile from here to Willis's," said Joseph, "and it ain't five score yards from theer to the Tan-yard. Theer's some," he added, with an almost philosophic air, "as knows when they are well off."

"I'll give you an extra penny," said his lordship, condescending to bargain.

"I'll do it for a extry sixpince," replied Joseph.

"I'll make it twopence," said his lordship—"twopence and a screw of snuff."

"I'll do it for a extry sixpince," Joseph repeated, doggedly.

Noblesse oblige. There was a point beyond which the Earl of Barfield could not haggle. He surrendered, but it galled him, and the agreeable sense of humor with which he commonly regarded Joseph Beaker failed him for the rest of that afternoon. It happened, also, that the people who remained to be encountered one and all opposed him, and with the exception of his triumph over the Widow Hotchkiss the day was a day of failure.

When, therefore, his lordship turned his steps homeward he was in a mood to be tart with anybody, and it befell that Ferdinand was the first person on whom he found an opportunity of venting his gathered sours. The young gentleman heaved in sight near the lodge gates, smoking a cigar and gazing about him with an air of lazy nonchalance which had very much the look of being practised in hours of private leisure. Behind him came the valet, bearing the big square color-box, the camp-stool, and the clumsy field easel.

"Daubing again, I presume?" said his lordship, snappishly.

"Yes," said Ferdinand, holding his cigar at arm's-length and flicking at the ash with his little finger, "daubing again."

His lordship felt the tone and gesture to be irritating and offensive.

"Joseph Beaker," he said, "take the ladder to the stables. I have done with you for to-day. Upon my word, Ferdinand," he continued, when Joseph had shambled through the gateway with the ladder, "I think you answer me with very little consideration, for—in short, I think your manner a little wanting in—I don't care to be addressed in that way, Ferdinand."

"I am sorry, sir," said Ferdinand. "I did not mean to be disrespectful. You spoke of my daubing. I desired to admit the justice of the term. Nothing more, I assure you."

His lordship, in his irritated mood, felt the tone to-be more irritating and offensive than before.

"I tell you candidly, Ferdinand, that I do not approve of the manner in which you spend your time here. If you imagine that you can walk over the course here without an effort you are very much mistaken. I take this idleness and indifference very ill, sir, very ill indeed, and if we are beaten I shall know on whom the blame will rest. The times are not what they were, Ferdinand, and constitutional principles are in danger."

"Really, sir," returned Ferdinand, "one can't be electioneering all the year round. There can't be a dissolution before the autumn. When the time comes I will work as hard as you can ask me to do."

"Pooh, pooh!" said his lordship, irritably. "I don't ask you to spout politics. I ask you to show yourself to these people as a serious and thoughtful fellow, and not as a mere dauber of canvas and scraper of fiddles. You come here," he went on, irritated as much by his own speech as by the actual circumstances of the case, "as if you were courting a constituency of *dilettanti*, and expected to walk in by virtue of your little artistic graces. They don't want a man like that. They won't have a man like that. They're hard-headed fellows, let me tell you. These South Stafford fellows are the very deuce, let me tell you, for knowing all about Free-trade, and the Cheap Loaf, and the National Debt."

"Very well, sir," said Ferdinand, laughing, "I reform. Instead of carrying easel and *porte-couleur,* Harvey shall go about with a copy of 'The Wealth of Nations,' and when a voter passes I'll stop and consult the volume and make a note. But *l'homme serieux* is not the only man for election times. I'll wager all I am ever likely to make out of politics that I have secured a vote this afternoon, though I have done nothing more than offer a farmer's wife a little artistic advice about the choice of a bonnet. I told her that yellow was fatal to that charming complexion, and advised blue. Old Holland is proud of his young wife, and I hooked him to a certainty."

"Holland!" cried his lordship, more pettishly than ever— "Holland is conservative to the backbone. We were always sure of Holland."

"Well, well," said Ferdinand, in a voice of toleration, "we are at least as sure of him as ever."

The allowance in the young man's manner exasperated the old nobleman. But he liked his young friend in spite of his insolence and tranquil swagger, and he dreaded to say something which might be too strong for the occasion.

"We will talk this question over at another time," he said, controlling himself; "we will talk it over after dinner."

"I must go vote-catching after dinner," returned Ferdinand. "I promised to go and listen to the quartette party this evening."

"Very well," returned his lordship, with a sudden frostiness of manner. "I shall dine alone. Good-evening."

He marched away, the senile nodding of his head accentuated into pettishness; and Ferdinand stood looking after him for a second or two with a smile, but presently thinking better of it, he hastened after the angry old man and overtook him.

"I am sorry, sir, if I disappoint you," he said. "I don't want to do that, and I won't do it if I can help it." The earl said nothing, but walked on with an injured air which was almost feminine. "Are you angry at my proposing to go to see old Fuller? I understood you to say yesterday that his vote was undecided, and that nothing was so likely to catch him as a little interest in his musical pursuits."

"I have no objections to offer to your proposal," replied his lordship, frostily—"none whatever."

"I am glad to hear that, sir," said Ferdinand, with rather more dryness than was needed. His lordship walked on again, and the young man lingered behind.

The household ways at the Hall were simple, and the hours kept there were early. It was not yet seven o'clock when Ferdinand, having already eaten his lonely dinner, strolled down the drive, cigar in month, bound for old Fuller's garden. He thought less of electioneering and less of music than of the pretty girl he had discovered yesterday. She

David Christie Murray

interested him a little, and piqued him a little. Without being altogether a puppy, he was well aware of his own advantages of person, and was accustomed to attribute to them a fair amount of his own social successes. He was heir to a baronetcy and to the estates that went with it. It was impossible in the course of nature that he should be long kept out of these desirable possessions, for the present baronet was his grandfather, and had long passed the ordinary limits of old age. The old man had outlived his own immediate natural heir, Ferdinand's father, and now, in spite of an extraordinary toughness of constitution, was showing signs of frailty which increased almost day by day. And apart from his own personal advantages, and the future baronetcy and the estates thereto appertaining, the young man felt that, as the chosen candidate of the constitutional party for that division of the county at the approaching election, he was something of a figure in the place. It was rather abnormal that any pretty little half-rustic girl should treat him with anything but reverence. If the girl had been shy, and had blushed and trembled before him a little, he could have understood it. Had she been pert he could have understood it. Young women of the rustic order, if only they were a trifle good-looking, had an old-established license to be pert to their male social superiors. But this young woman was not at all disposed to tremble before him, and was just as far removed from pertness as from humility.

As he strolled along he bethought him, vaguely enough—for he was not a young gentleman who was accustomed to put too much powder behind his purposes—that it would be rather an agreeable thing than otherwise to charm this young woman, if only just to show her that she could be charmed, and that he could be charming. He had been a little slighted, and it would be nice to be a little revenged. He was not a puppy, in spite of the fact that his head gave house-room to this kind of nonsense. The design is commoner among girls than boys, but there are plenty of young men who let their wits stray after this manner at times, and some of them live to laugh at themselves.

But while Ferdinand was thinking, an idea occurred to him which caused him to smile languidly. It would be amusing to awaken Barfield's wrath by starting a pronounced flirtation with this village beauty. It was scarcely consistent to have an inward understanding with himself, that if the flirtation *should* take place it should be kept secret from his noble patron of all men in the world. It would certainly be great fun to take the little hussy from her pedestal. She was evidently disposed to think of herself a good deal more highly than she ought to think, and perhaps it might afford a useful lesson to her to be made a little more pliant, a little less self-opinionated, a little less disposed to snub young gentlemen of unimpeachable attractions. Thinking thus, Ferdinand made up quite a contented mind to be rustic beauty's school-master.

The green door in the garden wall was still a little open when he reached it, but he could hear neither music nor voices.

The evening concert had not yet begun, and he was fain to stroll on a little farther. This of itself was something of an offence to his majesty, though he hardly saw on whom to fix it. He did not know his way round to the front of the house, and did not care to present himself at the rear unless there were somebody there to receive him. He lit a new cigar to pass away the time, and re-enacted his first and only interview with the girl he had made up his mind to subjugate. In the course of this mental exercise he experienced anew the sense of slight he had felt at her hands, but in a more piercing manner. He had spoken to her, and she had waved her hand against him as if he had been a child to be silenced. He had spoken to her again, and she had not even responded.

In point of fact she had ignored him. The more he looked at it the more remarkable this fact appeared, and the more uncomfortable and the more resolved he felt about it.

When his cigar was smoked half through he sighted the upright and stalwart figure of Reuben Gold, who was striding at a great pace towards him, swinging his violin-case in one hand. Ferdinand paused to await him..

"Good-evening, Mr. Gold," he said, as Reuben drew near.

"Good-evening," said Reuben, raising his eyes for a moment, and nodding with a preoccupied air. His rapid steps carried him past Ferdinand in an instant, and before the young gentleman could propose to join him he was so far in advance that it was necessary either to shout or run to bring him to a more moderate pace. Ferdinand raised his eye-glass and surveyed the retreating figure with some indignation, and dropped it with a little click against one of his waistcoat-buttons. Then he smiled somewhat wry-facedly.

"A cool set, upon my word," he murmured. "Boors, pure and simple."

He was half inclined to change his mind and stay away from the al fresco concert, but then the idea of the duty he owed himself in respect to that contumelious young beauty occurred to him, and he decided to go, after all. He followed, therefore, in Reuben's hasty footsteps, but at a milder pace, and, regaining the green door, looked into the garden and saw the quartette party already assembled. Old Fuller, who was the first to perceive him, came forward with rough heartiness, and shook hands with a burly bow.

"Good-evenin', Mr. De Blacquaire," said Fuller. "We're pleased to see you. If you'd care to tek a hand i'stead of settin' idle by to listen, we shall be glad to mek room. Eh, lads?"

"No, no, thank you, Mr. Fuller," said Ferdinand, "I would rather be a listener." Ruth was standing near the table, and he raised his cap to her. She answered his salute with a smile of welcome, and brought him a chair. "Good-evening, Miss Fuller," he said, standing cap in hand before her. "What unusually beautiful weather we are having. Do you know, I am quite charmed with this old garden? There is something delightfully rustic and homely and old-fashioned about it."

"You are looking at the statues?" she said, with half a laugh. "They are an idea of father's. He wants to have them painted, but I always stand out against that—they look so much better as they are."

"Painted?" answered Ferdinand, with a little grimace, and a little lifting of the hands and shrinking of the body as if the idea hurt him physically. "Oh no. Pray don't have them painted."

"Well, well. Theer!" cried Fuller. "Here's another as is in favor o' grime an' slime! It's three to three now. Ruth and Reuben have allays been for leavin' 'em i' this way."

"Really, Mr. Fuller," said Ferdinand, "you must be persuaded to leave them as they are. As they are they are charming. It would be quite a crime to paint them. It would be horribly bad taste to paint them!"

After this partisan espousal of her cause, he was a little surprised to notice an indefinable but evident change in the rustic beauty's manner. Perhaps she disliked to hear a stranger accuse her father—however truly—of horribly bad taste, but this did not occur to Ferdinand, who had intended to show her that a gentleman was certain to sympathize with whatever trace of refinement he might discover in her.

"Would it?" said Fuller, simply. "Well, theer's three of a mind, and they'm likely enough to be right. Anny ways theer's no danger of a brush coming anigh 'em while the young missis says 'No.' Her word's law i' this house, and has been ever since her was no higher than the table."

"Wasn't that a ring at the front door?" asked Sennacherib, holding up his hand.

"Run and see, wench," said Fuller.

Ruth ran down the grass-plot and into the house. She neither shuffled nor ambled, but skimmed over the smooth turf as if she moved by volition and her feet had had nothing to do with the motion. She had scarce disappeared, when Isaiah, who faced the green door, sung out,

"Here's Ezra Gold, and bringin' a fiddle, too. Good-evenin', Mr. Gold. Beest gooin' to tek another turn at the music?"

"No," said Ezra, advancing. "I expected to find Reuben here. I've got it on my mind as the poor old lady here "—he touched the green baize bag he carried beneath his arm—"is in a bit o' danger o' losin' her voice through keeping silence all these length o' years, and I want him to see what sort of a tone her's got left in her."

Reuben rose from his seat with sparkling eyes and approached his uncle.

"Is that *the* old lady I've heard so much about?" he asked.

"Yes," replied Ezra, "it's the old lady herself. I don't know," he went on, looking mildly about him, "as theer's another amateur player as I'd trust her to. Wait a bit, lad, while I show her into daylight."

Reuben stood with waiting hands while the old man unknotted the strings at the mouth of the green baize bag, and all eyes watched Ezra's lean fingers. At the instant when the knot was conquered and the mouth of the bag slid open, Ruth's clear voice was heard calling,

"Father, here's Aunt Rachel! Come this way, Aunt Rachel. We're going to have a little music."

CHAPTER VI

Ezra Gold, seizing the violin gently by the neck, suffered the green baize bag to fall to the ground at his feet, and then tenderly raising the instrument in both hands, looked up and dropped it to the ground. A little cry of dismay escaped from Reuben's lips, and he was on his knees in an instant.

"She's not hurt," he said, examining the violin with delicate care— "not hurt at all."

Then he looked up, and at the sight of his uncle's face rose swiftly to his feet. The old man's eyes were ghastly, and his cheeks, which had usually a hectic flush of color too clear and bright for health, were of a leaden gray. Ezra's hand was on his heart.

"Not hurt?" he said, in a strange voice. "Art sure she's not hurt, lad? That's fortunate."

The color came back to his face as suddenly as it had disappeared.

"No," said Reuben, tapping the back of the fiddle lightly with his finger-tips, and listening to the tone, though he kept his eyes fixed upon his uncle's—"she's as sound as a bell."

"That's well, lad, that's well," said Ezra, in the same strange voice. The hands he reached out towards his nephew trembled, and Reuben handed back the precious instrument in some solicitude. It was natural that an old player should prize his favorite instrument, but surely, he thought, a little chance danger to it should scarcely shake a man in this way. Ezra's trembling hands began to tune the strings, and at the sound of Ruth's voice Reuben turned away. His uncle's agitation shocked him. He had known for years, as everybody had known, that Ezra had but a weakly constitution, but he had never seen so striking a sign of it before, and the old man's agitation awoke the young man's fears. There was a very close and tender affection between them.

"Reuben," Ruth was saying, "this is my aunt Rachel. Aunt, this is Mr. Reuben Gold. I don't suppose you remember him."

"I do not remember Mr. Reuben Gold," said the little old lady, mincingly. "Is Mr. Gold a native of Heydon Hay? I do not think, from Mr. Gold's appearance, that he was born when I quitted the village. I think I recognize my old friends, the Elds," she went on, with an air almost of patronage. "This will be Mr. Isaiah? Yes! I thought so. Mr. Isaiah was always mild in manner. And this will be Mr. Sennacherib? Yes! Mr. Sennacherib was unruly. I recognize them by their expressions."

"You remember me, Rachel?" said Mr. De Blacquaire, who had been watching the old lady since her arrival. She turned her head in a swift, bird-like way, and fixed her curiously youthful eyes upon him for an instant. The withered old face lit up with a smile which so transfigured it that for the moment it matched the youth of her eyes.

"Is it possible!" she cried. "Mr. Ferdinand! The dear, dear child!" She seized one of his hands and kissed it, but he drew it away, and putting an arm about her shoulders, stooped to kiss her wrinkled cheek. "The grandson," she cried, turning on the others with an air of pride and tender triumph, "of my dear mistress, Lady De Blacquaire. I nursed Mr. Ferdinand in his infancy. I bore him to the font, and in my arms he received his baptismal appellation."

If she had laid claim to the loftiest of worldly distinctions she could scarcely have done it with a greater air of pride.

Ezra's tremulous fingers were still at work at the violin keys when Ruth addressed him.

"I dare say you know my aunt Rachel, Mr. Gold," she said. "Heydon Hay was such a little place five-and-twenty years ago that everybody must have known everybody."

"It was my privilege to know Miss Blythe when she lived here," said Ezra, looking up and speaking in a veiled murmur.

The little old lady started, turned pale, drew herself to her full height, and turned away. Sennacherib, who was watching the pair, drove out his clinched fist sideways with intent to nudge his brother Isaiah in the ribs, to call his attention to this incident as a confirmation of the history he had told the night before. He miscalculated his distance, and landed on Isaiah's portly waistcoat with such force that the milder brother grunted aloud, and, arising, demanded with indignation to know why he was thus assaulted. For a mere second Sennacherib was disconcerted, but recovering himself, he drew Isaiah on one side and whispered in his ear,

"I on'y meant to gi'e thee a nudge, lad. Dost mind what I tode thee about 'em? Didst tek note how they met?"

"Thinkest thou'rt th' only man with a pair of eyes in his head?" demanded Isaiah, angrily and aloud. Sennacherib, by winks and nods and gestures, entreated him to silence, but for a minute or two Isaiah refused to be pacified, and sat rubbing at his waistcoat and darting looks of vengeance at his brother. "Punchin' a man at my time o' life i' that way!" he mumbled wrathfully; "it's enough t' upset the systim for a month or more."

Nobody noticed the brethren, however, for the other members of the little party had each his or her preoccupation.

"Mr. Ferdinand," said Miss Blythe, turning suddenly upon the young gentleman, "I must seize this opportunity to ask what news there is of my dear mistress. I know that she is frail, and that correspondence would tax her energies too severely, but I make a point of writing to her once a week and presenting to her my respectful service."

She took his hand again as she addressed him, and Ferdinand noticed that it was icy cold. She was trembling all over and her eyes were troubled. He was just about to answer when a sharp twang caught his ear, and turning his head he saw Ezra in the act of handing the violin to Reuben.

"Have you got a fourth string, lad?" asked Ezra, speaking unevenly and with apparent effort; "this has gi'en way. I'm no hand at a fiddle nowadays," he added, with a pitiable smile, "or else there's less virtue in catgut than there used to be."

"They make nothing as they used to do," said Reuben. He had drawn a flat tin box from his pocket and had selected a string from it, when Rachel drew Ferdinand on one side.

"Let me bring you a chair, Mr. Ferdinand," she said. "We will sit here and you must tell me of my dear mistress."

"Stay here," said Ferdinand, "I will bring you a chair." He was not sorry to be seen in this amiable light. It was agreeable to bend condescendingly to his grandmother's attached and faithful servitor, and to be observed. There was a genuine kindliness in him, too, towards the little withered old woman who had nursed him in his babyhood, and had taught him his first lessons. He brought the chairs and sat down with his old nurse at the edge of the grass-plot at some little distance from the others.

"We will talk for a little time about my dear mistress," said Rachel, "and then I will ask you to take me away." She leaned forward in her chair, looking up at her companion and laying both hands upon his arm. "I cannot stay here," she went on, in a whisper. "There are reasons. There is a person here I have not seen for more than a quarter of a century. You have observed that I am sometimes a little flighty." She withdrew one of her hands and tapped her forehead.

"My dear Rachel!" said Ferdinand, in smiling protestation.

"Yes, yes," she insisted, in a mincing whisper, as if she were laying claim to a distinction. "A little flighty. You do no credit to your own penetration, dear Mr. Ferdinand, if you deny it. That person is the cause. I suffered a great wrong at that person's hands. Let us say no more. Tell me about my dear mistress."

The varnish of unconscious affectation was transparent enough for Ferdinand to see through. The little old woman minced and bridled, and took quaintly sentimental airs, but she was moved a great deal, though in what way he could not guess. He sat and talked to her with a magnificent unbending, and she took his airs as no more than his right, and was well contented with them.

"And now, Reuben," cried Fuller, who, like everybody else, had noticed Miss Blythe's curious behavior to Ezra and was disturbed by it—"and now, Reuben, if thee hast got the old lady into fettle, let's have a taste of her quality. It's maney an' maney a year now since I had a chance of listenin' to her. Let's have a solo, lad. Gi'e us summat old and flavorsome. Let's have 'The Last Rose o' Summer.'"

Reuben sat down, threw one leg over the other, and began to play. The evening was wonderfully still and quiet, but from far off, the mere ghost of a sound, came the voice of church-bells. Their tone was so faint and far away that at the first stroke of the bow they seemed to die, and the lovely strain rose upon the air pure and unmingled with another sound. Rachel ceased her emphatic noddings and her mincing whisper, and sat with her hands folded in her lap to listen. Ezra, with his gaunt hands folded behind him, stood with his habitual stoop more marked than common, and stared at the grass at his feet. Ruth, from her old station by the apple-tree, looked from one to the other. She had heard Sennacherib's story from her father, and her heart was predisposed to read a romance here, little as either of the actors in that obscure drama of so many years ago looked like the figures of a romance now. They had been lovers before she was born, and had quarrelled somehow, and had each lived single. And now, when they had met after this great lapse of years, the gray old man trembled, and the wrinkled old woman turned her back upon him. The music was not without its share in the girl's emotion. And there was Reuben, with manly head and great shoulders, with strength and masculine grace in every line of him, to her fancy, drawing the loveliest music from the long-silent violin, and staring up at the evening sky as he played. Ah! if Reuben and she should quarrel and part!

But Reuben had never spoken a word, and the girl, catching herself at this romantic exercise, blushed for shame, and for one swift second hid her face in her hands. Then with a sudden pretence of perfect self-possession, such as only a woman could achieve on such short notice, she glanced with an admirably casual air about her to see that the gesture had not been observed. Nobody looked at her. Her father and the two brothers were watching Reuben, Ezra preserved his old attitude, Ferdinand was fiddling with his eye-glass, and moving his hand and one foot in time to the music, and Rachel's strangely youthful eyes were bright with tears. As the girl looked at her a shining drop brimmed over from each eye and dropped upon the neat mantle of black silk she wore. The little old maid did not discover that she had been crying until Reuben's solo was over, and then she wiped her eyes composedly and turned to renew her conversation with Ferdinand.

"Ah!" said Fuller, expelling a great sigh when Reuben laid down his bow upon the table, "theer's a tone! That's a noble instrument, Mr. Gold."

"She'll be the better for being played upon a little," said Ezra, mildly.

"Well, thee seest," said Isaiah, with a look of contemplation, "her's been a leadin' what you might call a hideal sort o' life this five-and-twenty 'ear for a fiddle. Niver a chance of ketchin' cold or gettin' squawky. Allays wrapped up nice and warm and dry. Theer ain't, I dare venture to say it, a atom o' sap in the whole of her body. Her's as dry as—"

"As I be," interposed Sennacherib. "It 'ud be hard for anything to be drier. Let's have a drop o' beer, Fuller, and then we'll get to work."

Ruth ran into the house laughing, and the four musicians gathered round the table. Ferdinand arose, strolled towards them, and took up a position behind Sennacherib's chair. Ezra made an uncertain movement or two, and finally, with grave resolve, crossed the grass-plot and took the chair the young gentleman had vacated.

"I am informed, Miss Blythe," he said, with a slow, polite formality, "as you have come once more to reside among us." She inclined her head, but vouchsafed no other answer. The movement was prim to the verge of comedy, but it was plain that she meant to be chilly with him. He coughed behind his shaky white hand, and hesitated. "I do not know, Miss Blythe," he began again, with a new resolve, "in what manner I chanced to 'arn your grave displeasure. That is a thing I never knew." She turned upon him with a swift and vivid scorn. "A thing I never knew," he repeated. "If it is your desire to visit it upon me at this late hour, I have borne it for so many 'ears that I can bear it still. But I should like to ask, if I might be allowed to put the question, how it come to pass. I have allays felt as there was a misunderstandin' i' the case. It is a wise bidding in Holy Writ as says, 'Let not the sun go down upon thy wrath.' And when the sun is the sun of life the thing is the more important."

"My good sir," said Rachel, rising from her seat and asserting every inch of her small stature, "I desire to hold no communication with you now or henceforth."

"That should be enough for a man, Miss Blythe," said Ezra, mildly. "But why? if I may make so bold."

"I thought," said the little old lady, more starched and prim than ever, "I believed myself to have intimated that our conversation was at an end."

76 David Christie Murray

"You was not wont to be cruel nor unjust in your earlier days," Ezra answered. "But it shall be as you wish."

He left the seat, gave her a quaint old-fashioned bow, and returned to his former standing-place. Ruth was back again by this time, and Rachel crossed over to where she stood.

"Niece Ruth," she said, speaking after a fashion which was frequent with her, with an exaggerated motion of the lips, "I shall be obliged to you if you will accompany me to the house."

"Certainly, aunt," the girl answered, and placing an arm around her shoulders, walked away with her. "There is something the matter, dear. What is it?"

"There is nothing the matter," said the old lady, coldly.

"There is something serious the matter," said Ruth. They were in the house by this time, and sheltered from observation. "You are trembling and your hands are cold. Let me get you a glass of wine."

Aunt Rachel stood erect before her, and answered with frozen rebuke,

"In my young days girls were not encouraged to contradict their seniors. I have said there is nothing the matter."

Ruth bent forward and took the two cold, dry little hands in her own warm grasp, and looked into her aunt's eyes with tender solicitude. The hands were suddenly snatched away, and Aunt Rachel dropped into a seat, and without preface began to cry. Ruth knelt beside her, twining a firm arm and supple hand about her waist, and drawing down her head softly until its gray curls were pressed against her own ripe cheek. Not a word was spoken, and in five minutes the old maid's tears were over.

"Say nothing of this, my dear," she said, as she kissed Ruth, and began to smooth her ruffled ribbons and curls. Her manner was less artificial than common, but the veneer of affectation was too firmly fixed to be peeled off at a moment's notice. "We are all foolish at times. You will find that out for yourself, child, as you grow older. I have been greatly disturbed, my dear, but I shall not again permit my equilibrium to be shaken by the same causes. Tell me, child, is Mr. Ezra Gold often to be found here?"

"Not often," said Ruth; "he seems scarcely ever to move from home."

"I am glad to know it," said Aunt Rachel. "I cannot permit myself to move in the same society with Mr. Ezra Gold."

"We all like him very much," Ruth answered, tentatively.

"Ah!" said Aunt Rachel, pinching her lips and nodding. "You do not know him. *I* know him. A most despicable person. They will tell you that I am a little flighty."

"My dear aunt! What nonsense!"

"It is not nonsense, and you know it. I *am* a little flighty—at times. And I owe that to Mr. Ezra Gold. I owe a great deal to Mr. Ezra Gold, and that among it. Now, dear, not a word of this to anybody. Will you tell dear Mr. Ferdinand that I shall be honored if he will grace my humble cottage with his presence? Thank you. Good-night, child. And remember, not a word to anybody."

She dropped her veil and walked to the front door with her

usual crisp and bird-like carriage. At the door she turned.

"Shun Mr. Ezra Gold, my dear. Shun all people who bear his name. I know them. I have cause to know them. They are cheats! deceivers! villains!"

She closed her lips tightly after this, and nodded many times. Then turning abruptly she hopped down the steps which led towards the garden gate, and disappeared. Ruth stood looking into the quiet street a moment, then closed the door and returned to the garden.

"Not all," she said to herself, as she paused in sight and hearing of the quartette party, who were by this time deep in an andante of Haydn's—"not all."

CHAPTER VII

When Aunt Rachel had spent a fortnight or thereabouts in Heydon Hay, and had got her own small dwelling-place into precise order, she began to make a round of visits among the people she had known in her youth. She had met most of the survivors of that earlier day at the parish church on Sundays, and had had no occasion to find fault with the manner of her reception at their hands. If there was not precisely that warmth of greeting which she felt in her own heart, she found at least a kindly interest in her return and a friendly curiosity as to her past. To her, her return to her birthplace was naturally an event of absorbing interest. To the other inhabitants of the village it was no more than an episode, but nobody being distinctly cold or careless, Rachel was not allowed to see the difference between their stand-point and her own.

In her round of calls she left the house of Sennacherib Eld till the last, though she and Mrs. Sennacherib had been school-fellows and close friends. Perhaps she had not found Sennacherib's manner inviting, or perhaps the fact that Ezra Gold's house lay between her own and his had held her back a little. Everybody had supposed that she and Ezra Gold were going to be married six-and-twenty years ago, Rachel herself being among the believers, and having, it must be confessed, admirable ground for the belief. Nobody knew how the match had come to be broken off. It was so Old-world a bit of history that even in Heydon Hay, where history dies hard, it had died and been buried long ago. Even Rachel's return could not resuscitate it for more than one or two. But the story that was dead for other people was still alive to her, and as fresh and young—now that it was back in its native air again—as if it had been an affair of yesterday. It was something of a task to her to pass the house in which the faithless lover lived. It would be the first achievement of that feat since Ezra had treated her so shamelessly, and it was almost as difficult after six-and-twenty years as it might have been after as many days.

She clinched her lips tightly as she came in sight of the tall poplars which stood beyond the spire of the church, and rose to an equal height with it, and at the lich-gate of the church she paused a little, feigning to take interest in one or two tombstones which recorded the death of people she had known. Her troubled eyes took no note of the inscriptions, but in a while she found resolution Jo go on again. With her little figure drawn uncompromisingly to its fullest height, she rounded the corner of the church-yard and saw the familiar walls. Ezra, contrary to his habit, was standing at the side door and looking out upon the street. She was aware of his presence, but walked stiffly past, disregarding him, and he coughed behind his wasted hand. She thought the cough had a sound of embarrassed appeal or deprecation, as perhaps it had, but she refused to take notice of it, except by an added rigidity of demeanor.

Sennacherib's house stood back from the highway a hundred yards or so beyond Ezra's. It was fenced all round by an ill-trimmed hedge of hawthorn, and the only break in the hedge was made by the un-painted wooden gate which led by a brick-paved walk to the three brick steps before the door. The door stood open when Rachel reached it, and the knocker being set high up and out of reach, she tapped upon the wood-work with the handle of her sunshade. This summons eliciting no response, she repeated it; but by-and-by the opening of a door within the house let out upon her the sound of Sennacherib's voice, hitherto audible only as an undefined and surly buzz.

"Who's master i' this house?" Sennacherib was asking— "thee or me?"

"If brag and swagger could ha' made a man the master," said a feminine voice, in tones of feeble resignation, "theer's no doubt it's you, Sennacherib."

"Brag and swagger?" said Sennacherib.

"Lord o' mercy!" replied the feminine voice, "what do you want to shout a body deaf for? Brag and swagger was what I said, Sennacherib. But if you think as a mother's heart is agoing to be overcome by that sort o' talk, and as I shall turn my back upon my very own born child, you've fell into the biggest error of your lifetime."

Rachel rapped again somewhat louder than before.

"Canst choose betwixt that young rip and me," replied Sennacherib.

"That's right; let the parish know your hard-heartedness! Theer's somebody knockin' at the door. Go and tell 'em what you've made up your wicked mind to—do!"

Sennacherib thrust his head into the hall and stared frowningly at the visitor through his spectacles.

"Good-morning, sir," said Rachel, with frigid politeness. "I called for the purpose of paying my respects to Mrs. Eld. If the moment is inauspicious I will call again."

At the sound of her voice Mrs. Sennacherib appeared—a large woman of matronly figure but dejected aspect. She had been comely, but thirty years of protest and resignation had lifted the inner ends of her eyebrows and depressed the corners of her mouth until, even in her most cheerful moments, she had a look of meek submission to unmeasured wrongs.

"Dear me!" said Mrs. Sennacherib, sailing round her husband and down the hall, "it's Miss Blythe! Come in, my dear, and tek off your cloak and bonnet. I'm glad to see you. I wondered if you was never comin' to see me. And how be you?" She bent over the little figure of her guest and buried it in an embrace like that of a feather-bed. "It's beautiful weather for the time o' year," she continued, almost tearfully, "and I have been a-thinking of makin' a call upon you; but I'm short of breath, and Eld is such a creetur he'd rather see a body stop in the house as if it was a prison, than harness the pony and drive me half a mile, to save his life."

"Short o' breath!" said Sennacherib. "Thee talkest like one as is short o' breath! Her talks enough," he added, addressing the visitor, "to break the wind of a Derby race-hoss."

"Ah," said his wife, shaking her head in a kind of doleful triumph, "Miss Blythe won't ha' been long i' the village afore her'll know what manner o' man you be, Sennacherib."

"I'll leave thee to tell her," said Sennacherib, with a grunt of scorn. "If I'd ha' been the manner o' man you'd ha' liked for a husband, I *should* ha' been despisable. My missis"—he addressed his wife's visitor again—"ought to ha' married a door-mat, then her could ha' wiped her feet upon him wheniver the fancy took her."

With this he took his hat from a peg, stuck it at the back of his head, and marched out at the open front door.

"Ah, my dear," said Mrs. Sennacherib, "you did a wise thing when you made up your mind to be a single woman. The men's little more than a worrit—the best of 'em—and even the childern, as is counted upon for a blessin', brings trouble oftener nor j'y."

The visitor pinched her lips together and nodded, as if to say there was no disputing this glaring statement. The hostess, stooping over her, untied her bonnet-strings as if she had been a child, helped her to remove her mantle, and then ushered her into a sitting-room which looked upon a well-cultivated garden.

"I wouldn't say," pursued the hostess, "as I'd got a bad husband—not for the world. But he's that hard and unbendin' both i' little things an' big uns. I've suffered under him now for thirty 'ear, but I niver counted as he'd put the lad to the door and forbid his mother to speak to him. Though as for that, my dear, he may forbid and go on forbiddin' as long as theer's a breath in his body, but a mother's heart is a mother's heart, my dear, though the whole world should stand up again her."

"Precisely," said Rachel.

"The lad's just as unbendin' as his father," pursued Mrs. Sennacherib, "though in a lighter-hearted sort of a way. He's as gay as the lark, our Snac is, even i' the face o' trouble, but there's no more hope o' movin' him than theer'd be o' liftin' the parish church and carryin' it to market. He's gone and married again his father's will, and now his father's gone an' made his last dyin' testyment an' cut him off wi' a shilling. He'll get my money, as is tied on me hard an' fast, and that's my only comfort."

"They may be reconciled," said Rachel. "We must try to reconcile them."

"Reconcile Sennacherib Eld!" cried the wife, dolefully. "Ah, my dear, you don't know the man. Why, who's that? There's somebody a-walkin' in as if the house belonged to 'em."

A young man in a stand-up collar, and trousers supernaturally tight, appeared at the open door and nodded in a casual manner.

"Mornin', mother," said the young man, cheerfully. "Wheer's the governor?"

Mrs. Sennacherib screamed, and running at the new-comer began to embrace him and to kiss him and cry over him.

"Theer, theer!" he said, after kissing her off-hand. "Tek it easy."

"Oh, Snac!" cried his mother, "if father should come in what should we do?"

"Do?" said the younger Sennacherib, "why, set me down afore the kitchen fire, an' mek me happetizin' afore he sets to work to eat me. How be you, mum?"

The younger Sennacherib's face was gay and impudent, with that peculiar mingling of gayety and impudence which seems inseparable from freckles. His face was mottled with freckles, and the backs of his hands were of a dark yellowish brown with them.

"This is Miss Rachel Blythe," said his mother, "as was at school with me when I was a gell. This is my poor persecuted child, Miss Blythe."

"Me, mum!" said the persecuted child, standing with his feet wide apart, and bending first one knee and then the other, and then bending both together. "The governor's out, is he?"

"He's only just gone," returned his mother. "But, Snac, you'll only anger him, comin' in i' this way. You'd better wait a bit and let things blow over."

"Well," said Snac, "I shouldn't ha' come for any-thin' but business. But I've got a chance o' doin' a bit o' trade with him. He's had his mind set on Bunch's pony this two 'ear, an' Bunch an' him bein' at daggers drawn theer was niver a chance to buy it. But me an' him bein' split, old Bunch sells me the pony, and I called thinkin' he might like to have it."

He laughed with great glee, and flicked one tightly clad leg with the whip he carried.

"Wait a bit, Snac," his mother besought him. "Let it blow over a bit afore approachin' him."

"Wait for the Beacon Hill to blow over!" said Snac, in answer. "I've no more expectations as the one 'll blow over than th' other. He'll do what he says he'll do. That's the pattern he's made in. I've got no more hopes of turnin' the governor than I should have if I was to go and tell a hox to be a donkey. It's again his natur' to change, and nothing short of a merracle 'll alter him. But as for livin' at enmity with him—wheer's the use o' that? He's all the feythers I've got, or am like to find at my time o' life, and I must just mek the best on him."

"A most commendable and Christian resolution," said Rachel, decisively.

"Very nice and kind of you to say so, mum," Snac answered, setting his hat a little more on one side, and bending both knees with a rakish swagger. "You can tell the governor as I called, mother. The pony's as genuine a bit of blood as is to be found in Heydon Hay. The p'ints of a hoss and a dog is a thing as every child thinks he knows about, but bless your heart theer's nothing i' the world as is half so difficult t' understand, unless it is the ladies." There was such an air of compliment about the saving clause that Rachel involuntarily inclined her head to it. "You'll tell the governor as I was here, mother," Snac concluded, stooping down to kiss her.

"You mustn't ask me to do that, Snac," she answered. "I dar' not name your name."

"Rubbidge!" said Snac, genially. "Does he bite?"

"It's for your sake, Snac," said his mother, "not for mine. But I dar' not do it."

"Well, well, mayhap I shall light upon him i' the village. If I shouldn't, I'll look in again. Good-mornin', mother, and good-day to you, mum. I'm just goin' to drop in on Mr. Ezra Gold, seein' as I'm this way. I'm told he wants to part with that shorthorn cow of hisn, and I'm allays game for a bit o' trade."

"Ah!" said Mrs. Sennacherib, shaking her doleful head. "He'll part with everythin' earthly, poor man, afore he's much older."

"Why," cried Snac, "what's the matter with the man?"

"The young uns see nothin', Miss Blythe," said Mrs. Sennacherib, shaking her head again, but this time with a sort of relish. "But old experienced folks can tell when any poor feller-creetur's time is drawing nigh. His father went just at his time o' life by the same road as he's a-takin'."

"Well, what road is he takin'?" her son demanded.

"Look at his poor hands," said Mrs. Sennacherib, with a pitying gusto. "As thin as egg-shells, and with no more color in 'em than there is in that cha-ney saucer. Hark to that dry cough as keeps on a hack-hack-hackin' at him."

"Pooh!" cried young Sennacherib. "He's been like that as long as I can remember him."

"Mark my words," his mother answered, with a stronger air of doleful relish than before, "he'll niver be like that much longer."

"Theer's them as looks at the dark side," returned Snac, "and them as looks at the bright. Niver say die till your time comes. I'll go and wake him up a bit, though he's no great hand at a bargain, and seems to find less contentment in gettin' on the blind side of a man than most on 'em. Good-mornin', mother; good-mornin', mum."

Snac took his way with a flourish, and his mother looked after the tight-clad legs, the broad shoulders, the tall collar, and the rakish hat with mournful admiration.

"Do you think," asked the little old maid, coughing behind her hand, and looking out of window as she spoke, as if the theme had but little interest for her, "that Mr. Ezra Gold is really unwell?"

"Yes, my dear," said Mrs. Sennacherib; "he's got enough to last his time, unless it should please the Lord to send him a new and suddener affliction. I've seen a many go the same road. It's mostly the young as bears his particular kind of sufferin', but it's on his face in as plain readin' as the family Bible. He's a lonish sort of a man, save for his nephew Reuben, but he'll ha' the parish for his mourners when his time does come. The gentlest, harmlessest creetur as ever was a neighbor is Ezra Gold."

"Hem!" said Aunt Rachel. The monosyllable was at once curt and frozen. It implied as complete a denial as could have been expressed in a volume.

"Why, what have you got again him?" asked Mrs. Sennacherib.

"I?" said Rachel. "Against whom, my dear creature?"

Mrs. Sennacherib had spoken in the absolute certainty of impulse, and found herself a little confused.

"Mr. Gold," she answered, somewhat feebly.

"What should I have against Mr. Gold?" asked the old maid, with a chill air of dignity and a pretence of surprise. She was not going to take everybody into her confidence.

"What, to be sure?" said Mrs. Sennacherib, retiring from instinct. "In old days there used to be a sort of kindness between you; at least it was said so."

"It is a great pity that people cannot be taught to mind their own business," said Rachel.

"So it is, Miss Blythe—so it is," Mrs. Sennacherib assented, hastily. "I hate them folks as has got nothing better to do than to talk about their neighbors. But, as I was a-sayin', he's a-breakin' up fast, poor man, and that's a thing as is only too clear to a old experienced eye like mine. A beautiful sperrit the man's got, to be sure, but allays a mild and sorrowful look with him. When me and Sennacherib was first married, he'd a habit of coming over here with 'Saiah Eld and Mr. Fuller for the music. It was pretty to hear 'em, for they'm all fine players, though mostly theer music was above my mark; but sometimes they'd get him to play somethin' by himself, and then 'twas sweet. But he give up playin' all of a sudden —I could niver mek out why or wheer-for, an' I suppose it's over five-an'-twenty 'ear since he touched the fiddle."

Now Mrs. Sennacherib, though not an untruthful woman as a general thing, had an idea as to the why and wherefore of Ezra Gold's withdrawal from the amateur ranks of Heydon Hay. She took most of her ideas from her husband, though she was not accustomed to think so, and it was he who had inoculated her with this one. She laid her small trap for her old friend and school-fellow with an admirable nonchalance and indifference of aspect, and looked at Rachel with an eye from which all appearance of speculation was carefully abstracted.

"He gave up playing?" Rachel asked, with a tone of surprise.

"Yes," said Mrs. Sennacherib, with a stolid-seeming nod. "He give it up clean. Why, now I come to think on it, I don't believe he iver touched the music—" She paused in some confusion, and to cover this feigned to consider. "Let me see. He give up the music just about the time as you went away to Barfield."

The old maid's lips twitched, her cheeks went pale, and a look of absolute terror rose to her eyes.

"I was always under the impression that nothing could have induced him to give up his music. As I remember him he was peculiarly devoted to it."

She did her best to speak indifferently, but her voice shook in spite of her.

"He give it up just about the time as you went away," repeated Mrs. Sennacherib. "I've heard our Sennacherib and his brother 'Saiah say over and over again as since that time he niver so much as opened a piece of music."

The little old maid arose with both hands on her heart, tight-clasped there. Her eyes were wild and she panted as if for breath.

"Miss Blythe!" cried the other, alarmed by her aspect— "Rachel! What's the matter? Why, my dear, you're ill! A glass o' wine; me own mekin', my dear. Theer's no better elderberry i' the parish. Tek a drop, now do; it'll do you good, I'm sure."

"No, thank you," said Rachel, waving the proffered glass aside and sinking back into her chair. "It passes very soon. It is quite gone. I thank you. Pray take no notice of my ailments, Mrs. Eld. I am sorry, to have discommoded you, even for a moment."

She was her prim and mincing self again, though there was still a tremor in her voice, and the exalted look in her young eyes was more marked than common. After a little time she recovered herself completely, and Mrs. Sennacherib entertained her for an hour with mournful histories of death and burial. The good woman had a rare nose for an invalid and a passion for nursing. Such of her old school-fellows as had died since Rachel's departure had mostly been nursed out of life under the care of Mrs. Sennacherib, and she was intimate with the symptoms of all of them, from the earliest to the latest. There was but little need for Rachel to talk at all when once her hostess had entered upon this absorbing topic, and when the old maid arose to go she had altogether recovered from the effect of whatever emotion had assailed her.

She walked homeward so prim, so old, so withered, that ninety-nine in a hundred would have laughed to know that she was living in the heart of a love-story, and that story her own. But we rarely grow old enough to forget our own griefs, howsoever cold the frost of age may make us to the griefs of others.

CHAPTER VIII

The young Sennacherib, swaggering gayly from his unnatural parent's door, was aware of something as nearly approaching a flutter as not often disturbed the picturesque dulness of the village main street. By some unusual chance there were half a dozen people in the road, and not only did these turn to stare at him, but at least half a dozen others peered at him from behind the curtains of cottage interiors, or boldly flattened their noses against the bulbous little panes of glass in the diamonded windows.

"Theer's a look of summat stirrin' i' the place, gaffer," said Snac to one ancient of the village.

"Why, yis, Mr. Eld, theer is that sort of a air about the plaeas to-day," the old fellow answered, with a fine unconsciousness. "But then theer mostly *is* a bit of a crowd round our town pump."

The crowd about the town pump consisted of one slatternly small girl and a puppy.

"Can't a chap call on his feyther 'ithout the Midland counties turnin' out to look at him?" Snac asked, smilingly.

"Yis," returned the ancient, who was conveniently deaf on a

sudden. "Theer's been no such fine ripenin' weather for the wheat sence I wur a lad."

Snac gave the riding-whip he carried a burlesque threatening flourish, and the old boy grinned humorously.

"Sin Joseph Beaker this mornin', Mr. Eld?" he asked.

"No," said Snac. "What about him?"

"His lordship's gi'en him a set o' togs," said the old rustic, "an' he's drunker wi' the joy on 'em than iver I was with ode ale at harvest-time."

"Aha!" cried Snac, scenting a jest. "Wheer is he?"

"Why, theer he is!" said the rustic, and turning, Snac beheld Joseph Beaker at that moment shambling round the corner of the graveyard wall, followed closely by the youth of the village. The Earl of Barfield had kept his promise, and had bestowed upon Joseph a laced waistcoat—a waistcoat which had not been worn since the first decade of the century, and was old-fashioned even then. It was of a fine crimson cloth, and had a tarnished line of lace about the edge and around the flaps of the pockets. Over this glorious garment Joseph wore a sky-bine swallow-tail coat of forgotten fashion, and below it a pair of knee-breeches which, being much too long for him, were adjusted midway about his shrunken calves. A pair of hob-nailed bluchers and a battered straw hat gave a somewhat feeble finish to these magnificences. As the poor Joseph aired the splendors of his attire there was a faint and far-away imitation of the Earl of Barfield in his gait, and he paused at times after a fashion his lordship had, and perked his head from side to side as if in casual observation of the general well-being.

"Good-morning, Lord Barfield," cried Snac, as Joseph drew near. "It's a sight for sore eyes to see your lordship a-lookin' so young and lusty." Joseph beamed at this public crowning of his loftiest hopes, and would have gone by with a mere nod of lordly recognition but the triumph was too much for him and he laughed aloud for joy. "Well, bless my soul!" said Snac, in feigned astonishment, "it's Mister Beaker. Send I may live if I didn't tek him for the Right Honorable th' Earl o' Barfield! Thee'st shake hands with an old friend, Mr. Beaker? That's right. Theer's nothin' I admire so much as to see a man as refuses to be carried away with pride." Joseph shook hands almost with enthusiasm.

"Theer's nothin' o' that sort about me, Mr. Eld," he replied.

"That I'm sure on," said Snac, with conviction. "But how gay we be to-day, Mr. Beaker."

"It was my lord as gi'en me these," said Joseph, retiring a pace or two to display his raiment, and gravely turning round in the presence of the little crowd that surrounded him so that each might see the fulness of its beauty.

At this moment Reuben Gold came swinging along the road with a green baize bag under his arm. He was on his way to his uncle's house, and, unobserved of Snac, took a place on the causeway to see what might be the reason of this unusual gathering.

"Now," said Snac, "I never thought as Lord Barfield 'ud be so mean as to do things in that half-an'-half manner. I should ha' fancied, if Lord Barfield had took it into his head to set up an extra gentleman in livery, he'd ha' done it thorough."

Joseph's countenance fell, and he surveyed his own arms and legs with an air of criticism. Then he took hold of the gold-laced flaps of the crimson waistcoat and laughed with a swift and intense approval.

"Ain't this been done thorough?" he demanded.

"As far as it goes, Joseph," replied the jocular Snac, "it's noble, to be sure." Joseph became critical again, but again at the sight of the gold-laced waistcoat his doubts vanished. "But surely, surely, Joseph, he should ha' gi'en you a pair o' them high collars as he wears, and a cravat, to go along with a get out like that."

"He might ha' done that, to be sure," said Joseph, tentatively.

"Might ha' done it!" cried Snac, with a voice of honest scorn. "Ah! and would ha' done it if he'd been half a man, let alone a peer of the realm. For that's what he is, Joseph—a peer of the realm."

"So he is," said the poor Joseph, who was rapidly sliding into the trap which was set for him. "You would have expected a peer of the realm to do it thorough, wouldn't you?"

"Look here, Joseph," continued Snac, opening his trap wide, "you go and tell him. 'My lord,' says you—a-speakin' like a man, Joseph, and a-lookin' his lordship i' the face as a man in a suit of clothes like them has got a right to do—'my lord,' you says, 'you're as mean as you're high,' says you. 'What for?' says he. 'Why,' says you, 'for settin' a man out i' this half-an'-half mode for the folks to laugh at. Give me a collar and a cravat this minute, you says,' or else be ashamed o' thyself. Be ayther a man or a mouse.' That's the way to talk to 'em, Joseph."

"Think so?" asked Joseph, with an air half martial and half doubtful.

"To be sure," cried Snac; and with one exception everybody in the little crowd echoed "To be sure!"

"I'll goo an' do it," said Joseph, thus fortified, "this instant minute."

"Wait a bit Joseph," said Reuben Gold, "I'm going that way. We'll go a little of the road together."

"Now, Mr. Gold," cried Snac, in a whisper, recognizing Reuben's voice before he turned, "don't you go an' spoil sport."

"Snac, my lad," responded Reuben, smiling, "it's poor sport."

"He'd go an' tell him," said Snac, with a delighted grin. "You can mek him say annythin'."

"That's why it's such poor sport," said Reuben. "It's too easy. It's sport to stand up for a bout with the sticks when the other man's a bit better than you are, but it's no fun to beat a baby."

"I like it better," Snac replied, with candor, "when th' odds is on t'other side. I like to be a bit better than t'other chap."

"You like to win? That's natural. But you like to deserve a bit of praise for winning; eh?"

Reuben walked away with the rescued Joseph at his side. Joseph was as yet unconscious of his rescue, and was fully bent upon his message to the earl.

"Theer's no denyin' that chap nothin," said Snac, looking after Reuben's retiring figure. "He's got that form an' smilin' manner as'll tek no such thing as a no. An' lettin' that alone," he continued, again relapsing into candor, "he could punch my head if he wanted to, though I'm a match for ere another man i' the parish—and he'd do it too, at anny given minute, for all so mild as he is."

"He's the spit of what his uncle was," said the aged rustic. "When he was a lad he was the best cudgel-player, the best man of his hands, and the prettiest man of his feet from here to Castle Barfield."

"He's fell off of late 'ears, then," said Snac.

"Ah!" quavered the old fellow, "it's time as is too many for the best on us, Mr. Eld. Who'd think as I'd iver stood again all comers for miles and miles around for the ten-score yards? I did though!"

"Didst?" cried Snac. "Then tek a shillin' and get a drop o' good stuff wi' it, an' warm up that old gizzard o' thine wi' thinkin' o' thy younger days."

And away he swaggered, carrying his shilling's worth with him in the commendations of the rustic circle. He was a young man who liked to be well thought of, and to that end did most of his benefactions in the open air.

In the mean time Reuben had disappeared with Joseph, and was already engaged in spoiling the village sport. Joseph was so resolved upon the collars and the cravat, and his imagination was so fired by the prospect of those splendid additions to his toilet, that Reuben was compelled to promise them from his own stores. Joseph became at once amenable to reason, and promised to overlook his lordship's meanness.

"Are you going to do anything for his lordship to-day, Joseph?" his protector asked him.

David Christie Murray

"No," said Joseph. "He's gi'en me a holiday. I tode him as 'twarn't natural to think as a man 'ud want to go to work i' togs like thesen. The fust day's wear, and all!"

"Well, if you *should* care to earn a shilling—"

"I couldn't undertek a grimy job," said Joseph. "Not to-day. A message now."

"A message? Could you take the message in a wheelbarrow, Joseph?"

"A barrer?" Joseph surveyed his arms and legs, and then took a grip of the laced waistcoat with both hands.

"A message in a wheelbarrow for a shilling, and a pair of collars and a black satin cravat to come I home in, Joseph."

"Gaffer," said Joseph, "it's a bargain."

Reuben's message was Ezra Gold's musical library, and the volumes having been carefully built up in a roomy wheelbarrow, Joseph set out with them at a leisurely pace towards his patron's home. Reuben on first entering his uncle's house had laid the green baize bag upon the table. When the books were all arranged, and Joseph had started away with them, Reuben re-entered.

"I've brought the old lady back again, uncle," he said.

"You've eased her down, I hope, lad," said the old man, untying the bag and drawing forth the violin. "That's right. As for bringing her back again, you remember what used to be the sayin' when you was a child, 'Give a thing and take a thing, that's the devil's plaything.' I meant thee to keep her, lad. It's a sin an' a shame as such a voice should be silent."

"Uncle," said Reuben, stammering somewhat, "I scarcely like to take her. It seems like—like trespassing on your goodness."

"I won't demean th' old lady," returned Ezra. "Her comes o' the right breed to have all the virtues of her kind. Her's a Stradivarius, Reuben, and my grandfather gi'en fifty guineas for her in the year seventeen hundred an' sixty-one. A king might mek a present of her to a king. And that's why in the natural selfishness of a man's heart I kep' her all these 'ears hangin' dumb and idle on the wall here. I take some shame to myself as I acted so, for you might ha' had her half a dozen years ago, and ha' done her no less than as much justice as I could iver ha' done her myself at the best days of my life. Her's yourn, my lad, and I only mek one bargain. If you should marry and have children of your own, and one of 'em should be a player, he can have her, but if not, I ask you to will her to somebody as'll know her value, and handle her as her deserves."

Reuben was embarrassed by the gift.

"To tell the truth, uncle," he said, "I should take her the more readily if I'd coveted her less."

"Bring her out into the gardin, lad," returned his uncle. "Let's hear the 'Last Rose' again."

Reuben followed the old man's lead. His uncle's house-keeper carried chairs to the grass-plot, and there the old man and the young one sat down together in the summer air, and Reuben, drawing a little pitch-pipe from his pocket, sounded its note, adjusted the violin, and played. Ezra set his elbows upon his knees and chin in his hands, and sat to listen.

"Lend her to me, lad," he said, when his nephew laid the

David Christie Murray

instrument across his knees. "I don't know—I wonder—Let's see if there is any of the old skill left." His face was gray and his hands shook as he held them out. "Theer's almost a fear upon me," he said, as he took the fiddle and tucked it beneath his chin. "No, no, I dar' not. I doubt the poor thing 'ud shriek at me."

"Nonsense, uncle," answered Reuben, with a swift and subtle movement of the fingers of the left hand, such as only a violin-player could accomplish. "I doubt if there is such a thing as forgetting when once you have played. Try."

"No," said the old man, handing back the fiddle. "I dar' not. I haven't the courage for it. It's a poor folly, maybe, for a man o' my years to talk o' breakin' his heart over a toy like that, and yet, if the tone wasn't to come after all! That 'nd be a bitter pill, Reuben. No, no. It's a thousand to one the power's left me, but theer's just a chance it hasn't. I feel it theer." The gaunt left-hand fingers made just such a strenuous swift and subtle motion as Reuben's had made a minute earlier. "And yet it mightn't be." Reuben reached out the violin towards him, but he recoiled from it and arose. "No, no. I dar'n't fail," he said, with a gray smile. "I darn't risk it. Take her away, lad. No, lend her here. A man as hasn't pluck enow in his inwards for a thing o' that kind—Lend her here!"

He seized the instrument, tucked it once more beneath his chin, and with closed eyes laid the bow upon the strings. His left foot, stretched firmly out in advance of the right, beat noiselessly upon the turf, as if it marked the movement of a prelude inaudible except to him. Then the bow gripped the strings, and sounded one soft, long-drawn, melancholy note. A little movement of the brows, a scarcely discernible nod of the head marked his approval of the tone, and after marking anew the cadence of that airy prelude he began to play. For a minute or more his resolve and excitement carried him along, but suddenly a note sounded false and he stopped.

"Ah-h-h!" he cried, shaking his head as if to banish the sound from his ears, "take her, Reuben, take her. Give her a sweet note or two to take the taste o' that out of her mouth. Poor thing! Strike up, lad—anything. Strike up!"

Reuben dashed into "The Wind that Shakes the Barley!" and Ezra, with his gaunt hands folded behind him, walked twice or thrice the length of the grass-plot.

"Theer's no fool like an old fool," he said, when he paused at his nephew's side. "Theer's nothing as is longed for like that as can niver be got at. Good-day, lad. Tek her away and niver let anybody maul her i' that fashion again, poor thing. I'll rest a while. Good-day, Reuben."

Reuben thus dismissed shook hands and went his way, bearing his uncle's gift with him. His way took him to Fuller's house, and finding Ruth alone there he displayed his treasure and spent an hour in talk. If he had said then and there what he wanted to say, the historic Muse must needs have rested with him. But since, in spite of the promptings of his own desire, the favorableness of the time, and the delightful confusions of silence which overcame both Ruth and himself in the course of his visit, he said no more than any enthusiast in music might have said to any pretty girl who was disposed to listen to him, the historic Muse is free to follow Joseph Beaker, with whom she has present business.

In the ordinary course of things Joseph would have taken the shortest cut to his patron's house, but to-day neither the weight of the barrow-load, which was considerable, nor Joseph's objection to labor, which was strongly rooted, could prevent him from taking the lengthier route, which lay along the village main street, and therefore took him where he had most chance of being observed. He made but slow progress, being constantly stopped by his admirers, and making a practice of sitting down outside any house the doors of which happened to be closed, and there waiting to be observed. Despite the lingering character of his journey he had already passed the last house but one—Miss Blythe's cottage—and was forecasting in the dim twilight of his mind the impression he would make upon its inmate, when the little old maid herself went by without a glance.

"Arternoon, mum," said Joseph, setting down the wheelbarrow, and spitting upon his hands to show how little he was conscious of the glory of his own appearance.

"Good-afternoon," said the old maid. "Ah! Joseph Beaker?" To Joseph's great disappointment she took no notice of his attire, but her eye happening to alight upon the books, she approached and turned one of them over. Poor Joseph was not accustomed to read the signs of emotion, or he might have noticed that the hand that turned the leaves trembled curiously. "What are these?" she asked. "Where are you taking them?"

"These be Mr. Ezra Gold's music-books," he answered. "He's gi'en 'em to his nevew, and I'm a-wheelin' of 'em home for him. Look here—see what his lordship's gi'en to me."

But Miss Blythe was busily taking book after book, and was turning over the leaves as if she sought for something. Her hands were trembling more and more, and even Joseph thought it odd that so precise and neat a personage should have let her parasol tumble and lie unregarded in the dust.

"Wheel them to my house, Joseph Beaker," she said at last, with a covert eagerness. "I want to look at them; I should like to look at them."

"My orders was to wheel 'em straight home," returned Joseph. "I worn't told to let nobody handle 'em, but it stands to rayson as they hadn't ought to be handled."

"Wheel them to my door," said the little old maid, stooping for her fallen sunshade. "I will give you sixpence."

"That's another matter," said Joseph, sagely. "If a lady wants to look at 'em theer can't be nothin' again that, I *should* think."

The barrow was wheeled to Miss Blythe's door, and Miss Blythe in the open air, without waiting to remove bonnet, gloves, or mantle, began to turn over the leaves of the books, taking one systematically after the other, and racing through them as if her life depended on the task. Rapidly as she went to work at this singular task, it occupied an hour, and when it was all over the prim, starched old lady actually sat down upon her own door-step with lax hands, and crushed her best new bonnet against the door-post in a very abandonment of lassitude and fatigue.

"Done?" said Joseph, who had been sitting on the handle of the wheelbarrow, occasionally nodding and dozing in the pleasant sunlight. Miss Blythe arose languidly and gave him the promised sixpence. "You'm a wonner to read, you be, mum," he said, as he pocketed the coin. "I niver seed none on 'em goo at sich a pace as that. Sometimes my lord 'll look at one side of a noospaper for a hour together. I've sin him do it."

Receiving no reply, he spat upon his hands again, and started on the final course of his journey. Rachel closed the gate behind him, and walked automatically into her own sitting-room.

"There is no fool like an old fool," she said, mournfully. Then, with sudden fire, "I have known the man to be a villain these six-and-twenty years. Why should I doubt it now?"

And then, her starched dignity and her anger alike deserting her, she fell into a chair and cried so long and so heartily that at last, worn out with her grief, she fell asleep.

CHAPTER IX

The church-bells made a pleasant music in Hey-don Hay on Sunday mornings, and were naturally at their best upon a summer Sunday, when the sunshine had thrown itself broadly down to sleep about the tranquil fields. Heydon Hay was undisturbed by the presence of a single conventicle in opposition to the parish church, and the leisurely figures in the fields and lanes and in the village street were all bent one way. In fine weather the worshippers were for the most part a little in advance of time, and thereby found opportunity to gather in knots about the lich-gate, or between it and the porch, where they exchanged observations on secular affairs with a tone and manner dimly tempered by the presence of the church.

Half a dozen people in voluminous broadcloth were already gathered about the lich-gate when Fuller appeared, carrying his portly waistcoat with a waddle of good-humored dignity, and mopping at his forehead. He was followed by a small boy, who with some difficulty carried the 'cello in a big green baize bag. One or two of the loungers at the gate carried smaller green bags, and while they and Fuller exchanged greetings, Sennacherib and Isaiah appeared in different directions, each with a baize-clothed fiddle tucked beneath his arm. The church of Heydon Hay boasted a string band of such excellence that on special occasions people flocked from all the surrounding parishes to listen to its performances. The members of the band and choir held themselves rather apart from other church-goers, like men who had special dignities and special interests. They had their fringe of lay admirers, who listened to their discussions on "that theer hef sharp," which ought to have sounded, or ought not to have sounded, in last Sunday's anthem.

Whether his lordship made a point of it or not, the Barfield carriage was always a little late, and Ferdinand certainly approved of the habit; but on this particular morning the young gentleman was earlier than common and arrived on foot. The male villagers took off their hats as he walked leisurely along, the female villagers bobbed courtesies at him, and the children raced before him to do him a sort of processional reverence. This simple incense was pleasant enough, for he had spent most of his time in larger places than Heydon Hay, and had experienced but little of the sweets of the territorial sentiment. He walked along in high good-humor, and enjoyed his triumphal progress, though he made himself believe that it was only the quaint, rural, and Old-world smack of it which pleased him.

Here and there he paused, and was affable with a county elector, but when he reached the lich-gate he was altogether friendly with Fuller and Sennacherib, and shook hands with Isaiah with actual warmth.

"Mr. Hales was dining at the Hall last night," he said. "He told us that some of the local people were in favor of an organ for the church, and had talked about getting up a subscription, but he wouldn't listen to the idea."

"Should think not," said Sennacherib. "Parson knows when he's well off."

"Indeed he does," returned Ferdinand; "he looks on the band as being quite a part of the church, and says that he would hardly know the place without it."

"A horgin!" grunted Sennacherib, scornfully. "An' when they'd got it, theer's some on 'em as 'ud niver be content till they'd got a monkey in a scarlit coat to sit atop on it."

"I hardly think they want *that* kind of organ, Mr. Eld," said Ferdinand, smoothly.

"I do' know why they shouldn't," returned Sennacherib. "It's nothin' but their Christian humbleness as could mek 'em want it at all. The Lord's made 'em a bit better off than their neighbors, an' they feel it undeserved. It's castin' pearls afore swine to play for half on 'em about here."

Fuller, with both hands posed on the baize-clad head of the 'cello, which the small boy had surrendered to him some moments before, shook his fat ribs at this so heartily that Sennacherib himself re laxed into a surly grin, and then Ferdinand felt him self at liberty to laugh also.

"You are rather severe upon your audience, Mr. Eld," he said.

"A tongue like a file, our Sennacherib's got," said the mild Isaiah. "Touches nothin' but what he rasps clean through it."

Ferdinand raised his hat at this moment and made a forward step, with his delicately gloved right hand extended.

"Good-morning, Miss Fuller."

Mr. De Blacquaire prided himself, and not without reason, on his own *aplomb* and self-possession, but he felt now a curious fluttering sensation to which he had hitherto been an entire stranger.

Ruth accepted his proffered hand and responded to his salute, and then shook hands with the two brethren. Ferdinand, with a jealousy at which he shortly found time to be surprised, noticed that her manner in shaking hands with these two stout and spectacled old vulgarians differed in no way from her manner in shaking hands with him. This in itself was a renewal of that calm, inexplicable disdain with which the girl had treated him from the first. If rustic beauty had been fluttered at his magnificent pressure, he could have gone his way and thought no more about it; but when rustic beauty was just as cool and unmoved by his appearance as if their social positions had been reversed, the thing became naturally moving, and had in it a lasting astonishment for leisure moments.

And there was no denying that the girl was surprisingly pretty. Prettier than ever this Sunday morning, in a remarkably neat dress of dove color, a demurely coquettish hat, and a bit of cherry-colored ribbon. Rustic beauty was not altogether disdainful of town-grown aids, it would seem, for Ferdinand's eye, trained to be critical in such matters, noted that the girl was finely gloved and booted.

Her dress was like a part of her, but that, though the young gentleman could not be supposed to know it, was a charm she owed to her own good taste and her own supple fingers. The young gentleman might have been supposed to know, perhaps, that her greatest charm of all was her unconsciousness of charming, and it was certainly this which touched him more than anything else about her.

There was no outer sign of the young Ferdinand's inward disturbance.

"I am afraid," he said, resolute to draw her into talk with himself if he could, though it were only for a moment, "I am afraid that I have made Mr. Eld very angry."

Ruth's brown eyes took a half-smiling charge of Sennacherib's surly figure.

"Seems," said Sennacherib, "the young gentleman was a-dinin' last night along with the vicar, and it appears as some o' the fools he knows want to rob the parish church o' the band, and build a horgin."

"The vicar won't listen to the idea," said Ferdinand. "There was only one opinion about it."

"It would be a great shame to break up the band," Ruth answered, speaking with vivacity, and addressing Ferdinand. "Everybody would miss it so. We would rather have the band than the finest organ in the world."

It happened, as such things will happen for the disturbance of lovers, that just as Ruth turned to address Ferdinand, Reuben Gold marched under the lich-gate and caught sight of the group. The girl, her father, the two Elds, and the young gentleman were standing by this time opposite the church porch, but as far away from it as the width of the pathway would allow. Various knots of villagers, observing that his lordship's guest had stayed to talk, stood respectfully apart to look on, and, if it might be, to listen. Now Reuben, for reasons already hinted at, disliked Mr. De Blacquaire. He was not, perhaps, quite so conscious as Mr. De Blacquaire himself that all the advantage of the differences between them rested on the young gentleman's side. Reuben was not the sort of youngster who says to himself, "I am a handsome fellow," or "I am a clever fellow," or "I am a fellow of a good heart," but in face of Ferdinand's obvious admiration of

David Christie Murray

Ruth and his evident desire to stand well in her graces he had sprung up at once to self-measurement, and had set himself shoulder to shoulder with the intruder for purposes of comparison. With all the good the love for a good woman does us, with all the wheat and oil and wine it brings for the nourishment of the loftier half of us, it must needs bring a foolish bitter weed or two, which being eaten disturb the stomach and summon singular apparitions. And when Reuben saw the girl of his heart in vivacious public talk with a young man of another social sphere he was quite naturally a great deal more perturbed than he need have been. The gentleman admired her, and it was not outside the nature of things that she might admire the gentleman. He came up, therefore, mighty serious, and shook hands with Fuller and the brethren, and then with Ruth, with an air of severity which was by no means usual with him. He carried his violin case tucked beneath his arm—a fact which of itself gave him an unworthy aspect in Ferdinand's eyes—and he had shaken hands with Ruth without raising his hat. A denizen of Heydon Hay who had taken off his hat in the open air to a woman would have been scoffed by his neighbors, and would probably have startled the woman herself as much as his own sense of propriety. But all the same Reuben's salute seemed mutilated and boorish to the man of more finished breeding, and helped to mark him as unworthy to be the suitor of so charming a creature as the rustic beauty.

"Mr. De Blacquaire's a-tellin' us, Reuben," said old Fuller, "as theer's been some talk o' breaking up the church band and starting a horgin i' the place on it."

"That will end in talk," said Reuben, with a half-defiant, half-scrutinizing look at Ferdinand, as if he charged him in his own mind with having suggested the barbarism.

"There is no danger that it will go further in the vicar's time," returned Ferdinand. "Besides, his lordship is as strongly opposed to the change as anybody."

"It's time we was movin' inside, lads," said Fuller, glancing up at the church clock. Ruth inclined her head to Ferdinand, gave a nod and a smile to Reuben (who nodded back rather gloomily), and passed like a sunbeam into the shadow of the porch. Fuller took up his 'cello in a big armful, and followed, with the brethren in his rear. Ferdinand, feeling Reuben's company to be distasteful, lingered in it with a perverse hope that the young man might address him, and Reuben stood rather sullenly by to mark his own sense of social contrast by allowing the gentleman to enter first.

Each being disappointed by the other's immobility and quiet, a gradual sense of awkwardness grew up between them, and this was becoming acute when Ezra appeared, and afforded a diversion. Under cover of his uncle's arrival Reuben escaped into the church.

In the course of centuries the church-yard had grown so high about the building that grass waved on a level with the sills of the lower windows, and the church was entered by a small flight of downward steps. The band and choir had a little bare back gallery to themselves, and approached it by a narrow spiral stone staircase. There were no side galleries, and band and choir had therefore an uninterrupted survey of the building. Reuben valued his place because it gave him a constant sight of Ruth, and perhaps, though the fancy is certain of condemnation at the hands of some of the severer sort, the visible presence of the maiden, for whose sake he hoped for all possible excellences in himself, was no bad aid to devotion. She sat in a broad band of tinted sunlight with her profile towards her lover, looking to his natural fancy as if she caused the sunlight, and were its heart and centre. Opposite to her and with *his* profile towards the music gallery also, sat Ferdinand, and Reuben saw the young gentleman cast many glances across the church in Ruth's direction. This spectacle afforded no aid to devotion, and not even his music could draw the mind or eyes of the lover from Ferdinand, whom he began to regard as being an open rival.

There was enough in this reflection to spur the most laggard of admirers into definite action, and before the service was over Reuben had made up his mind. He would speak to Ruth after church, and at least decide his own chances. The vicar's sermon was brief, for the good man had no rival, and could afford to please himself; but its duration, short as it was, gave Reuben ample time to be rejected and accepted a score of times over, and to gild the future with the rosiest or cloud it with the most tempestuous of colors. The Earl of Barfield, according to his custom, had arrived late, and it comforted Reuben a little to think that in his presence, at all events, the young gentleman could make no progress with his love affairs. It comforted him further to see that Ruth took no notice of the glances of her admirer, and that she was to all appearance unconscious of them and of him.

But when once he had made up his mind to instant action, the vicar's brief discourse began to drag itself into supernatural length. Facing the preacher, and immediately beneath Reuben's feet, was a clock of old-fashioned and clumsy structure, and the measured tick, tick of its machinery communicated a faintly perceptible jar to a square foot or so of the gallery flooring. The mechanical rhythm got into Reuben's brain and nerves until every second seemed to hang fire for a phenomenal time, and the twenty minutes' discourse dragged into an age. Even when the vicar at last lifted his eyes from the neatly ranged papers which lay on the pulpit cushion before him, laid down his glasses, and without pause or change of voice passed on to the benediction, and even when after the customary decent pause the outward movement of the congregation began, Reuben's impatience had still to be controlled, for it was the duty of the band to play a solemn selection from the works of some old master while the people filed away. Reuben led, and since the others must needs follow at the pace he set, the old master was led to a giddier step than he had ever danced to in a church before. Sennacherib was scandalized, and even the mild Fuller was conscious of an inward rebellion. The taste in Heydon Hay was rather in favor of drawl than chatter, and the old masters in their serious moods were accustomed to be taken with something more than leisure.

"Why, Reuben, lad," began Sennacherib, "how didst come to let your hand run away with your elber i' that way?"

But Reuben, sticking his hat on anyhow, was gone before the old man had finished his question, thrusting his violin into its case as he made his way down the corkscrew stairs. A single glance assured him that Ruth was no longer in the churchyard. The Earl of Barfield's carriage blocked the way at the lich-gate, and the young fellow waited in high impatience until the obstacle should disappear. His lordship, in view of the approaching election, was much more amiable and talkative than common, and he and his protege stood exchanging talk upon indifferent topics with a little crowd of church-goers, but in a while the earl climbed slowly into the carriage. Ferdinand skipped nimbly after him and the two were driven away. Reuben, with hasty nods and good-mornings at one or two who would have detained him, strode into the highway just in time to see the dove-colored dress turn at a distant corner. He hurried after it at his swiftest walk, and reaching the corner in the most evident violent hurry, narrowly escaped walking over the object of the chase, who had halted in talk with Aunt Rachel at the place where their homeward ways divided.

David Christie Murray

He had expected to find her still far ahead, and this sudden encounter was amazingly disconcerting to him. To begin with, apart from his real purpose he had no business whatsoever round that particular corner. Then to pause suddenly in the midst of so violent a hurry was in itself a plain proclamation of his intent, and his hot courage had so rapidly gone cold that the change of inward temperature carried a shock with it. Nevertheless, he stopped and stammered a disjointed greeting to Rachel, who returned for sole answer an icy little nod, pinching her lips together somewhat superciliously as she gave it.

Ruth, who would have been burdened by a shyness equalling Reuben's own had he succeeded in catching her by herself, was bold enough in the presence of one of her own sex, and observed the situation with a delighted mischief. But this was changed, as swiftly as Reuben's emotions themselves, to a state of freezing discomfort when Aunt Rachel bolt upright, and with a mincing precision in her speech, demanded to know if this young—ahem!—this person had any communication to make.

"My dear aunt," said the poor girl, blushing scarlet, and casting an appealing glance at Reuben.

"You appeared to be in a hurry, Mr. Gold," said the terrible old lady. "My niece and I will not detain you."

"Thank you," responded Reuben, shaken back into self-possession. "I am not in a hurry any longer."

Aunt Rachel turned right about face with an almost military precision, and passing her arm through Ruth's led the girl away, leaving Reuben shaken back into internal chaos. Ruth's blushing face and humid brown eyes were turned towards him in momentary but keen apology, and he was left standing alone on the cobbled pavement with a feeling of perfect wreck.

"Aunt Rachel!" said the girl, as she suffered herself thus ignominiously to be towed away. "How could you make me behave so rudely?"

"Have nothing to do with those people," replied Aunt Rachel, frigidly. "They are bad, root and branch. I know them, my dear. That young man has the audacity to admire you. You must not encourage him."

"I am sure," said Ruth, guiltily, only half knowing what she said, "he has never spoken a word—"

"It is not necessary to wait for words," returned the old lady. "I can see quite clearly. I am experienced. I know the Golds. I have been familiar with the method of their villany for many years."

"How can you speak so?" the girl asked, recovering something of her native spirit. "I am sure that there is no better man in the world than Mr. Ezra Gold. Everybody speaks well of him."

"It is not quite accurate, my dear," said Aunt Rachel, "to say that everybody speaks well of him, when a person even so inconsiderable as myself is in the act of speaking ill of him." The quaint veneer of fashion with which for many years she had overlaid her speech and manner was more apparent in this address than common, but suddenly she broke through it and spoke with an approach to passion. "I know them; they are villains. Have nothing to do with any member of that family, my dear, as you value your happiness." She pinched her niece's arm tightly as she spoke, and for a little time they walked on in silence, Ruth not knowing what to say in

116   David Christie Murray

answer to this outburst, but by no means convinced as yet of the villany either of Ezra or Reuben. "Now, my dear," Aunt Rachel began again, with a return to her customary mincing tones, "you are not far from your own residence. I observe," with a swift glance over her shoulder, "that the person still lingers at the corner. But if he should attempt to follow you may rely upon me to intercept him. My niece must act like my niece. You must show your detestation of his odious advances in a proper manner."

"But, Aunt Rachel!" protested Ruth, "he has never made any advances, and I—I haven't any detestation."

"All in good time, my dear," responded the old lady. "In the mean time, rely upon my protection." With this she stood up birdlike, and pecked affectionately at Ruth's rosy cheek. The girl was well-nigh crying, but restrained herself, and answered Rachel's "God bless you" with some self-possession.

"Good-morning, dear aunt. But you are quite, oh, quite mistaken."

"Indeed, my dear," said Aunt Rachel, with a glitter in her youthful eyes, and a compression of her mobile lips, "I am nothing of the kind." Ruth's eyes sank, and she blushed before the old lady's keen and triumphant smile. She moved away downcast, while Aunt Rachel took the opposite direction. The old lady wore a determined air which changed to a sparkling triumph as she saw Reuben cross the road with an inelastic step, and continue his homeward way with a head bent either in thought or dejection.

CHAPTER X

When Reuben found time to gather himself together and to face his own emotions he discovered himself to be more amazed than disconcerted. He cast about in his mind for an explanation of the old lady's displeasure, and found none. Why should she desire to insult him? In what possible way could he have offended her? Even a lover (ingenious as lovers always are in the art of self-torment) could not persuade himself that Ruth was a willing party to her aunt's singular treatment of him. The apology in her glance had been unmistakable.

He was altogether at a loss to understand in what way he could have excited Miss Blythe's anger, but it was unpleasant to know that there was an enemy in the camp which he had always thought entirely friendly. With the exception of Ruth herself he had been sure of the approval of everybody concerned.

His performance at the homely one o'clock dinner spread at his mother's table was so poor as to be noticeable, and he had to endure and answer many tender but unnecessary inquiries as to the state of his health, and to pretend to listen while his mother related the melancholy history of a young man who fell into a decline and died through mere neglect of meal-times. When this narrative was over and done with he escaped to his own room, carrying writing materials with him, and sat down to express on paper the hopes he had fully meant to express vocally an hour earlier. The golden rule for writing is to know precisely what you want to say, but though Reuben seemed to know, he found it hard to get upon paper. Half a score of torn sheets went into the fire-grate, and were there carefully fired and reduced to ashes. It was only the discovery that he was reduced to his final sheet of paper which really screwed his courage to the sticking-point. Being once there it held until the need for it was over; but when the letter was written it would have followed its forerunners if there had but been another sheet of paper in the house or the day had been anything but Sunday. As it was, he let it stand perforce, enveloped and addressed it in a sort of desperation, and put it in his pocket ready for personal delivery. The quartette party always met on Sunday afternoons and played sacred music. Not so long ago they had been used to meet in church; but since the introduction of gas to the venerable building the afternoon service had been abandoned and an evening service instituted in its stead. The music-parties were held at Fuller's in the summer-time, and Reuben's chance of a declaration by letter looked simple and easy enough. It was but to slip the all-important note into Ruth's hand with a petition to her to read it, and the thing was done. He had time enough to do this over and over and over again in fancy as he walked down the sunlit street with his violin case tucked under his arm. He had time enough to be accepted and rejected just as often—to picture and enjoy the rapture of the one event and the misery and life-long loneliness entailed by the other. Every time his eager fancy slipped the note into Ruth's fingers his heart leaped and his hands went hot and moist, but if ever the screw of courage gave a backward turn the thought of Ferdinand twisted it back to the sticking-point again, and he was all resolve once more. The experience of ages has declared that there is no better spur for the halting paces of a laggard lover than that which is supplied by jealousy. The simplest coquette that ever tortured hearts in a hay-field is aware of the fact, and needs no appeal to the experience of ages to support her.

Reuben pushed the green gate aside, and entering upon the lawn, found Fuller in the act of carrying the table to its customary place. He had been so free of the house, and had been for years so accustomed to enter it and leave it at his will, that there was nothing in the world but his own restraining sense of shyness to prevent him from walking past his host with the merest salutation and fulfilling his own purpose then and there. But the trouble was that to his own disturbed feeling Fuller would infallibly have guessed his purpose, and either of the other members of the quartette arriving, or any chance visitor strolling in, would have known in a moment that he could have no other reason for entering the house than to ask Ruth's hand in marriage. So he stood somewhat awkwardly by the table, while Fuller re-entered the house and, after a little pause, returned with a pile of music.

"This here's one of Ezra's books, I reckon," said the elder, singling one volume from the pile. "It's the one you browt here the day he gi'en you his libery."

"Ah!" said Reuben, "Manzini? That was the last music he opened for his own playing, so he told me." He fluttered the leaves, glancing towards the house meanwhile, but seeing nothing of his goddess. Fuller contented himself with a mere grunt in answer to Reuben's statement, and rolled off into the house once more, returning this time with his 'cello. He prop-ped the instrument tenderly against the table, and, seating himself near it, began to arrange the music. Reuben still stood awkwardly fingering the leaves of Manzini's duets, when Ruth appeared at the house door. He had made but a step towards her, and had not even made a step in his mind towards reading the half-shy, half-appealing aspect she wore, when the prim figure of Aunt Rachel appeared from behind her, and the old woman, with defiance expressed in every line and gesture, laid her mit-tened hand on the girl's arm and advanced by her side. Reuben stood arrested, and made a bow which he felt to be altogether awkward. Ruth's brown eyes drooped, and she blushed, but she found courage a second or two later for a glance of appeal which Reuben did not see. He offered chairs to the old woman and the young one as they came near him, but Rachel, with a stony little nod, walked by, taking her niece with her.

The young man took instant counsel with himself. He sat down near the table with Manzini's oblong folio in his lap, and, turning the pages here and there, selected a moment when he was unobserved, and slipped his missive between the front board of the binding and the first blank leaf. It would be strange if he could not find time to whisper, "Look in Manzini" before the day was over; and even if that course should fail he could at least forward his letter by the penny-post, though that would imply a delay of twelve hours, and was hardly tolerable to think of. If he missed the opportunity for that hasty whisper he would carry Manzini away, and so re-secure possession of his letter.

While he was planning thus, Rachel and her niece were walking up and down the grass-plot, and the old lady was talking away at a great rate, describing the glories of the house of Lady De Blacquaire, and affecting to be absorbed in her theme. She was not so much absorbed, however, that her manner did not clearly indicate her misliking sense of Reuben's nearness every time she passed him, though she did not so much as cast a glance in his direction. By-and-by the two Elds appeared, and the customary business of the afternoon began. Reuben had much ado to pin himself down to the music, but he succeeded fairly well, and gave nobody reason to suppose that his mind wandered far and often from his task. It was well for his repute for sanity, especially after the wild leadership at morning service, that he was familiar with the theme. Even when his thoughts wandered farthest he was mechanically accurate. All the time the book with the all-important missive in it lay on the table before him, and in his fancy disasters were constantly happening which revealed his secret. He repeated the terms of the note again and again, and added to it and altered it and resolved to rewrite it, and again resolved to leave it as it was.

The afternoon party received an unusual addition in the persons of Mrs. Sennacherib and Mrs. Isaiah, who arrived when the performers were half-way through their programme.

"I forgot to tell thee, Reuben, lad," said Fuller, "Ruth's got a bit of a tay-party this afternoon, and thee beest to stop with the rest on 'em."

"Thank you," said Reuben; "I shall stay with pleasure." He felt Rachel's disapproving glance upon him, and looking up met it for a moment, and returned it with a puzzled gravity. She was standing alone at a little distance from the table, and Ruth and the two new arrivals were in the act of entering the house. Reuben obeyed the impulse which moved him, and rising from his place crossed over to where the little old lady stood. "May I ask," he said, "how I came to fall under your displeasure, Miss Blythe?" He glanced over his shoulder to assure himself that nobody took especial note of him, and spoke in a low and guarded voice.

Miss Blythe made the most of her small figure, glanced with extreme deliberation from his eyes to his boots and back again, and, turning away, followed her niece and the two new arrivals, walking with an air of exaggerated dignity. Reuben, returning to his seat, had to make great play with his pocket-handkerchief to cover the signs of confusion which arose at this rebuff. Miss Blythe could scarcely have expressed a livelier contempt for him if he had been a convicted pick-pocket.

His share of the music went so ill after this that he excited something like consternation in the minds of his friends.

"What's come to the lad, 'Saiah," asked Sennacherib.

"Bist a bit out o' sorts, Reuben, bisent?" said Isaiah, mildly anxious.

"I can't play to-day," Reuben answered, almost fretfully. "Let us try again. No. There's nothing the matter. Nothing in the world. Let us try again."

They tried again, and by dint of great effort Reuben kept control over himself and escaped further disgrace, although at one time Ruth's sympathetic, shy look almost broke him down, and at another, Rachel's stony gaze so filled him with wonderment and anger that he had much ado to save himself from falling.

Ruth retired to superintend the preparation of the tea-table within-doors, and Rachel followed her. In their absence he got on better, but it was almost as great a relief as he had ever known to find that the concert at last was over, and that he could give unrestrained attention to the thoughts which pressed upon him.

"Tea is ready," said Ruth, standing in the doorway, and shading her eyes from the afternoon sunlight with one hand. Rachel surveyed the quartette party from the window, but Reuben could see that she was held in talk by Mrs. Sennacherib.

"This may be my only chance to-day," said the lover to himself, with one great heart-beat and a series of flutterings after it. He controlled himself as well as he might, and with a single glance towards Ruth stood a little behind the rest and feigned to arrange the music on the table.

Isaiah and Sennacherib went first, and Fuller waddled in their rear. Reuben, after as long a pause as he dared to make, followed them, and raising his eyes saw that Ruth stood just without the door-way making room for her guests to pass. "Would she give him a chance for a word? The girl saw the unconscious pleading in his eyes, and blushing, looked on the ground. But she kept her place, and Reuben coming up to her just as Fuller's burly figure rolled out of sight through the door of the sitting-room, took both her hands in his, not knowing in his eagerness that he dared to advance so far, and murmured,

"Ruth, look in the Manzini. The duets. The book my uncle gave me."

"Niece Ruth," said Rachel's voice from the sitting-room door-way. Reuben dropped the hands he held, becoming conscious in that action only of the fact that he had taken them, and stepped into the dusky passage, thankful for the gloom, for he felt that he was blushing like a boy. Ruth had made a guilty start forward into the garden, and did not pause until she had reached the table. "I beg your pardon, sir," said Rachel, frostily, as she moved aside to make room for Reuben to pass her, but when she had once seen the young people wide apart she was satisfied, and forbore to call the girl again.

"Look in the Manzini," Reuben had said, and the girl, almost without knowing it, had paused with her hands resting on the glazed brown mill-board which bound it. He would think, if she opened the book at once, that she was curiously eager to obey him, and her heart told her pretty truly what she would find when she looked there. The fear almost made her turn away; but then, since she was there, if she did not care to look he would think her cruelly disdainful. Was anybody watching her? In every nerve she felt the eyes of all the party in the sitting-room as if they actually pierced and burned her. But standing with bent head, with an attitude of reverie which she felt to be unspeakably guilty, she raised the board with an air of chance, a semblance of no interest touching her features—as though that could influence anybody, since her face was hidden—and saw a letter with her name upon it. To lay one hand upon this, and to slip it into the pocket of her dress while actually turning with a look of nonchalance towards the sitting-room window, was felt by the criminal herself to be the most barefaced and wickedest of pretences. To make the tour of the garden afterwards with the letter in her pocket, and to gather flowers for a bouquet for the tea-table, while tea was actually ready and everybody was awaiting her, was at once a necessity, an hypocrisy, and a dreadful breach of good-manners.

She took her place at the tea-table with perfect innocence and unconsciousness of aspect; but Reuben looked guilty enough for two, until the genuine gravity of the situation recalled him to himself, when he began to look as solemn as a graven image, and returned wry answers to the talk of those about him. There was no calling back his declaration now, and he felt it to be clumsy beyond expression, and inadequate alike to his sense of Ruth's perfections and his own poor deserts. No man can quite know, until he has tried it, how severe an ordeal it is to sit at table with the lady of his heart, while that lady has his declaration, as yet unread, in her pocket.

Ruth was so self-possessed and tranquil that it was evident to her lover's masculine understanding that she was ignorant of the nature of his missive, and probably indifferent to it. Reuben's anxiety and preoccupation were in themselves a gladness to the girl, for they bore out the delightful prophecy of her own heart. She had always thought Reuben, even when she was a school-girl, the handsomest and manliest and cleverest of men. If it were unmaidenly to have thought so, and to allow her heart to be captured by a man who had never spoken a word of open love to her, she must be called unmaidenly. But there was never a purer heart in the world, and the sophistications of experience, vicarious or otherwise, had not touched her. It came natural to love Reuben, and perhaps the young man's eyes had made more of an excuse for her than would readily be fancied by those who have never experimented.

It may be, if the truth were known, that the maiden found the situation almost as trying as her lover, for there was a most tantalizing element of uncertainty in it, and uncertainty is especially grievous to the feminine heart. But at last her duty as hostess no longer severely holding her, she left the room, ostensibly to assist in clearing away the tea-things, and was no sooner out of sight than she skimmed like a swallow to her own chamber and there read Reuben's letter. When she came back again Reuben knew that she had read it, and knew, too, that she had read it with favor and acceptance. There was a subtle, shy, inward happiness in Ruth's heart which diffused itself for her lover's delight as if it had been a perfume. Not another creature but himself and her knew of it, and yet to him it was real, and as evident as anything he saw or touched.

Once or twice she looked at him so sweetly, so shyly, so tenderly, and yet withal so frankly, that his heart ached with the desire he felt to rise and clasp her in his arms and claim her for his own before them all. Aunt Rachel looked at him once or twice also, as if she stabbed him with an icicle, but he glanced back with a smile sunny enough to have thawed the weapon if only the bearer of it had been within measurable distance.

Rachel did not read her niece, for the simple reason that she was too resolved on reading what she supposed herself to have written to be able to trace the characters of mere nature. But she partly read the young man's triumph, and adjudged it as a piece of insolence, determining that he should be punished for it richly, as he deserved. She had exposed the character of the Golds to her niece, and had told her that they were wicked and bad and shameless—male jilts, whose one delight it was to break feminine hearts. Ruth would certainly believe what she had been told on such unimpeachable authority, and would never dream of permitting herself to be duped by a man of whom she knew so much beforehand. Any airs of triumph the young man might display were therefore ridiculous and insolent, deserving both of chastisement and contempt.

Ruth's household occupations took her away a second time, and if she chose to fill a mere two or three minutes by writing a note to a young man who sat within six yards of her, nobody suspected her of being so engaged. When she came back to her visitors, Reuben would fain have made opportunity to be near her, but Rachel was unwinking in her watchfulness, and he was compelled to surrender his design. The bells began to ring for evening church, and Ruth and the womenfolk went up-stairs to make ready for out-of-doors. The quartette party sat downstairs with open windows, each of the three seniors pulling gravely at a long church-warden, and the junior pretending to look at an old-fashioned book of beauty, in which a number of impossible ladies simpered on the observer from bowers of painted foliage.

Sitting near the window with his back to the garden, and

deeply absorbed in his own fancies, he found himself on a sudden impelled to turn his head, not because of any sound that reached him, but because of some curious intuition of Ruth's neighborhood to him. She was walking towards him at that moment, her footsteps falling soundlessly on the greensward, her face blushing and her eyes downcast. As she passed him and entered the house she raised her eyes for a moment, and Reuben read in them a sweet, enigmatical intelligence, and a charmed shyness so delicious that he thrilled at it from head to feet.

He longed, as any lover may imagine of him, to exchange a word with her. He was certain, but he desired to be more than certain. To know was nothing—his heart demanded to hear the good news and to be surfeited with hearing. But the small dragon still guarded his Hesperides, and on the way to church he escorted Mrs. Isaiah, a matron gaunt and stern, whose cheerful doctrine it was that any spoken word not made actually necessary by the business of life was a sin. Mrs. Isaiah's grim reticence was less of a trouble to him than it would have been under ordinary circumstances, for he had his own thoughts to think, and did not care to be drawn away from them.

At the lich-gate Aunt Rachel paused to shake hands with everybody but Ruth and Reuben.

"You had better take Manzini home to-night, Reuben," said Ruth. She tried hard to make her voice commonplace; but to Reuben's ears there was a meaning in it, and his eyes answered to the meaning with such a flash of tenderness and assured joy that, in spite of all she could do, Ruth must needs lower her head and blush again.

Rachel's youthful eyes flashed from one to the other.

David Christie Murray

"I do not propose to attend the service this evening, Niece Ruth," she said, a minute later, when Reuben and his *confrere* had entered on the cavernous darkness of the winding stairway. "I will call for you, however," she added. "I shall be in the porch at the close of the service."

At the first clause of this speech Ruth rejoiced, but at the second her sense of relief was spoiled.

"Very well, dear," she answered. Aunt Rachel could not stand much longer between her and Reuben, and if a fight should have to be made it would be early enough to begin it when she had her father definitely on her side, as she would have to-morrow. So she went into church and made strenuous efforts to attend to the service and the sermon, and failed dismally, and thought herself terribly profane.

Aunt Rachel, being left alone at the church porch, turned away and walked straight back to the house she had left. The green door in the high wall needed no more than a push to open it, and Rachel entered the garden, and, walking straight to the table at which the quartette party had sat playing an hour or two earlier, laid hands upon Manzini's volume of duets for the violin. She took it by the back of the cover and gave it a shake, and out from its pages fell a neatly folded little note, addressed in her niece's hand to Mr. Reuben Gold, and sealed in bronze wax with the impress of a rose. The little old lady pounced upon it, and held it at arm's-length in both hands.

"Infatuated child!" she said, in her primmest and most fashionable accent. "My premonitions have not deceived me."

She placed the note in the bosom of her dress, set the book in its former position upon the table, and left the garden.

Nobody looking at her could have supposed that she had been guilty of such an act; for if ever conscious rectitude and high resolve for good shone in a human face, they lighted hers. Once she stopped short in the lonely lane, and stamped one small foot with lofty emphasis.

"The very method!" she said aloud, in a voice of scorn. "For aught I know, the very book! You shall not suffer as I have suffered, my poor dear child. I thank Heaven that I am at hand to preserve you."

Thus animated by her own self-approval, Aunt Rachel, sometimes in scorn, sometimes in tenderness, but of tener in triumph, walked homeward, waited the due time, and walked back to church again. She succeeded in getting Ruth away without a sight of Reuben, but the young man passed them on their way with a step still quicker than he had used that morning. He threw a gay "good-night, Ruth," over his shoulder as he walked, and Ruth felt the old lady's hand tighten on her arm, though she was far from guessing the nature of the emotion which moved her.

Once out of sight in the summer dusk, Reuben ran. He reached the green door, and with no surprise found it wide open. He approached the table, seized the old folio? and turning it back downward so that nothing could fall from it, sped home, hugging it by the way. When he reached his own room he was breathless, but he struck a light, drew down the blinds, and turned over the leaves of the music-book one by one. In the centre of the book he paused, for there he seemed to find the object of his search. A note, bearing for sole superscription "Mr. Gold," was pinned to the edge of the page. But was that quaint, old-fashioned handwriting Ruth's? Why should she write to him on paper so old and yellow and faded? Why should the very pin that held it to the page be rusted as if it had been there for years?

The note was sealed with two wafers, and the paper cracked across as he opened it. It began "Dear Mr. Gold," and was signed "R." It ran thus—

"I have not ansrd your estmd note until now, though in receipt of it since Thursday, for I dare not seem precipitate in such a matter. But I have consulted my own heart, and have laid it before the Throne, knowing no earthly adviser. Dear Mr. Gold, it shall be as you wish, and I trust God may help me to be a worthy helpmeet. So no more till I hear again from you."

It was impossible that this should be meant for him, or that Ruth should have written it; but though he searched the book from cover to cover, there was no other missive to be found within it.

CHAPTER XI

"That is a very insolent young man," said Aunt Rachel, as Reuben threw his hurried greeting over his shoulder in the dusk.

"Indeed, aunt," the girl answered, a little more boldly than she would have dared to speak had the light been clearer— "indeed, aunt, you are quite mistaken about him, and I don't understand why you should speak of Mr. Gold and his uncle as you do."

She cared less what Rachel thought or said of Reuben's uncle, though she had always had a friendly and admiring friendship for the old solitary, than she cared what was thought and said of Reuben. But it was easier to champion the two together than to defend her lover alone.

"You are a child," said Aunt Rachel, composedly. "What do you know of the opposite sex?"

The question was obviously outside the range of discussion, but it silenced Ruth for the moment. The elder woman presumed upon her triumph, and continued:

"Confidence is natural to youth. That is an axiom I have frequently heard fall from the lips of my dear mistress. As you grow older you will grow less positive in your opinions, and will be careful to have a solid foundation for them. Now I know these people, and you do not."

"My dear aunt," said Ruth, in protest, "I have known Mr. Gold ever since I could walk."

"Of which Mr. Gold are we speaking?" demanded Rachel.

"It is true of both of them," Ruth answered. "Neither of them would harm a fly, or go a hair's-breadth from the truth for all the world. They are the best men I have ever known."

"Niece Ruth!" said Rachel, stopping short in her walk, and bringing Ruth to a halt also, "upon the only occasion, since my return to Heydon Hay, on which I have found myself in the society of Mr. Ezra Gold, I took you into my confidence with respect to him. That is to say, I took you into my confidence as much as I have ever taken anybody. Mr. Ezra Gold is a mean and hypocritical person. Mr. Ezra Gold is a person who would not stop at any act of baseness or cruelty. Mr. Ezra Gold is a villain."

All this came from the old maid's lips with a chill and prim precision, which troubled her hearer more than any heat or violence could have done. But the old man's face and figure were before her with a wonderful vivid clearness. The stoop was that of fatigue, and yet it had a merciful mild courtesy in it too, and the gray face was eloquent of goodness.

"I can't believe it!" cried the girl, warmly. "Dear aunt, there must have been some terrible mistake. I am sure he is a good man. You have only to look at him to know that he is a good man."

"A whited sepulchre," said Aunt Rachel, walking on again.

She had kept her mittened hand upon the girl's arm throughout the pause in their walk, and her very touch told her that Ruth was wounded and indignant. "What I say, I say of my own knowledge. He is a deliberate and a cruel villain."

The girl contained herself and was silent. In a little while she began to think with an almost tragic sense of pity of the withered and lonely old maid who walked beside her. She could pity thus profoundly because she could image herself in the like case; and though the figure she saw was far from being clear, her own terror of it and revolt from it told her how terrible it was. If she and Reuben should part as her aunt and Ezra had parted—if she should ever come to think of Reuben as Aunt Rachel thought of Ezra! The thought touched her with an arctic sense of cold and desolation. She drew away from it with an inward shudder, and in that instant of realization she saw the little old maid's personality really and truly standing in the middle of that bleak and frost-bound barrenness which she had dreamed as a possibility for herself. For the first time she saw and understood, and anger and bewilderment were alike swept away in the warm rush of sympathetic pity.

The road was lonely, and Ruth, with both eyes brimming over, placed her arm about her aunt's neck, and, stooping, kissed her on the cheek. Two or three of the girl's tears fell warm on Rachel's face, and the old maid started away from her with a sudden anger, which was less unreasonable than it seemed. She had of late years had an inclination to linger in talk about the theme of woman's trust and man's perfidy. For Ruth, and for Ruth only, she had identified this theory of hers with a living man who was known to both, but she had never intended herself to be pitied. She had never asked for pity in insisting that a righteous judgment should be dealt out to Ezra Gold. She had cried in Ruth's presence after her meeting with Ezra, but she had persuaded herself that her

David Christie Murray

tears resulted from nothing more than the shock she felt at meeting an old repulsion. And since she had got to believe this, it followed as a thing of course that Ruth ought also to have believed it. The girl's pity wounded her and shamed her.

"Thank you," she said, in her chillest and primmest fashion, as she withdrew from Ruth's embrace. "I am not in want of pity." It was in her mind to tell Ruth to beware lest she herself should be in need of pity shortly; but she suppressed herself at considerable cost, and walked on stiffly and uncomfortably upright.

"I am very sorry, dear," said Ruth. "I did not mean to hurt you."

But Rachel was very indignant, and it was only as she remembered the purloined letter that she consented to be appeased. After all, she had taken the girl's welfare in hand, and had interested herself so kindly in her niece's behalf that she could not bear to be angry with her. So she permitted a truce to be called, and on Ruth's renewed apologies asked graciously that no more should be said about the matter. They parted at the green door of the garden, and Rachel, walking homeward, pondered on one important question. Ought she or ought she not to know the contents of the letter? Without knowing them, how could she know exactly the length to which her niece and the intending worker of her ruin had already gone together? It was necessary to know that, and she slid her hand into the bosom of her dress, and held the letter there, half resolving to read it on her arrival at home. But although, as her theft of the letter itself would prove, her ideas of honor were quaint, they were strong. She had constituted herself Niece Ruth's guardian, and she meant to fulfil all her self-imposed duties to the letter, but there was one whose rights came before her own. The letter should be opened in the presence of Ruth's father, and the two authorities should consult together as to what might be done.

She cast about for a safe and unsuspicious resting-place for the letter, and at last decided upon the tea-caddy.

She placed it there, locked it up, and by the aid of a chair and a table stowed it securely away in the topmost corner of a tall cupboard. Then, having hidden the key in the parlor chimney, she went to bed and to sleep, profoundly convinced that she had adopted the wisest of possible courses, and that Niece Ruth would be saved in the morning.

Meantime Aunt Rachel's antique griefs being out of sight for Ruth, were out of mind. She had her own affairs to think of, and found them at once pressing and delightful. By this time Reuben would have read her note, and would know all it had to tell him. When she thought how much it told him it seemed daring and strange, and almost terrible that she should have written it. For it admitted that his letter had made her very happy; she was not quite sure that she had not written "very, very happy," and wished it were to write again. But here in the solitude of her own chamber she could kiss Reuben's letter, and could rest it against her hot cheek in an ecstasy of fluttering congratulations. How he looked, how he walked, how he talked, how he smiled, how he played! How brave, how handsome, how altogether noble and good and gifted he was! There was nobody to compare with him in Heydon Hay, and the young men of Castle Barfield were contemptible by comparison with him. A human sun before whose rays other young women's luminaries paled like rush-lights! She seemed to have loved him always, and always to have been sure that he loved her; and yet it was wonderful to know it, and strange beyond strangeness to have told. She fancied him in the act of reading her letter, and she kissed his as she did so. Did he kiss hers? Was he as glad as she was?

At these audacious fancies she hid herself and blushed.

Reuben all this while, and until a much later hour, was bewildering himself about the curious and old-fashioned missive he had discovered between the melodious pages of Manzini. Over and over again he searched through the volume, though he had already turned it leaf by leaf and knew that there was no chance of his having overlooked anything. Almost as often as he turned over the leaves of the music-book he reread the note he had taken from it. He questioned himself as to the possibility of his having allowed Ruth's note to fall, and mentally retraced his own fashion of taking up the book, and step by step the way in which he had carried it home. He was sure that nothing could have escaped from its pages since he had laid hands upon it, and was confronted with a double mystery. How had this time-stained epistle found its way into the pages, and how had the more modern missive be had fully expected to find there found its way out of it?

Suddenly an idea occurred to him which, though sufficiently far-fetched, seemed as if it might by chance explain the mystery. Long and long ago a son of the house of Gold had married a daughter of the house of Fuller. It was not outside the reasonable that Ruth should have had possession of this old document, in which a Ruth of that far-distant day had accepted a member of his own household. She might have chosen to answer him by this clear enigma, but a sense of solemnity in the phrasing of the letter made him hope his guess untrue. Desperate mysteries ask naturally for desperate guesses, and Reuben guessed right and left, but the mystery remained as desperate as ever. His thoughts so harried him that at last, though it was late for Heydon Hay, he determined to go at once to Fuller's house and ask for Ruth.

He slipped quietly down-stairs, and, leaving the door ajar,

walked quickly along the darkened road, bearing poor Rachel's long-lost letter with him; but his journey, as he might have expected, ended in blank disappointment. Fuller's house was dark. He paced slowly home again, refastened the door, and went to bed, where he lay and tossed till broad dawn; and then reflecting that he would catch Ruth at her earliest household duties, fell asleep, and lay an hour or two beyond his usual time.

But if Reuben were laggard the innocent guardian dragon was early astir. Fuller, in his shirt-sleeves and a broad-brimmed straw hat, was pottering about his garden with a wheelbarrow and a pair of shears. He saw her at the open door of the garden, and sang out cheerily,

"Halloo, Miss Blythe! Beest early afoot this mornin'. I'm a lover o' the mornin' air myself. Theer's no time to my mind when the gardin-stuff looks half as well. The smell o' them roses is real lovely."

He gave a loud-sounding and hearty sniff, and smacked his lips after it. Rachel seemed to linger a little at the door.

"Come in," said Fuller, "come in. There's nobody here as bites. Beest come to see Ruth? I doubt if her's about as yet. We ode uns bin twice as early risin' as the young uns, nowadaysen. Wait a bit and I'll gi'e her a bit of a chi-hike. Her'll be down in a minute."

"No," said Rachel, "don't call her. I do not wish to see her yet. It will be necessary to see her later on; but first of all I desire to speak to you alone." Fuller looked a little scared at this exordium, but Rachel did not notice him. He had never known her so precise and picked in air and speech as she seemed to be that morning, and through all this a furtive air of embarrassment peeped out plainly enough for even him to become aware of it. "May we sit down at this table?" she asked. "I presume the chairs are aired already by the warm atmosphere of the morning? There is no danger of rheumatism?"

"What's up?" inquired Fuller, sitting down at once, and setting his shirt-sleeved arms upon the table. "Theer's nothin' the matter, is theer?"

"You shall judge for yourself," replied Rachel. She drew a letter from her pocket, and covering it with her hand laid it on the table. A distinct odor of tea greeted Fuller's nostrils, and he noticed it even then. "I presume that you are not unacquainted with the character of the Messrs. Gold?"

"It 'ud be odd if I warn't acquynted with 'em," said Fuller. "I've lived i' the same parish with 'em all my days."

"That being so," said Rachel, "you will be able to appreciate my feelings when I tell you that almost upon my first arrival here I discovered that the younger Gold was making advances to my niece Ruth."

"Ah?" said Fuller, interrogatively. "I don't count on bein' able to see no furder through a millstone than my neighbors, but I've been aweer o' that for a day or two."

"Ruth is motherless," pursued Rachel, a little too intent upon saying things in a predetermined way to take close note of Fuller. "A motherless girl in a situation of that kind is always in need of the guidance of an experienced hand."

"Yis, yis," assented Fuller, heartily. "Many thanks to you, Miss Blythe, for it's kindly meant, I know."

"Last night," said Rachel, "I made a discovery." There was

nothing in the world of which she was more certain than she was of Fuller's approving sanction. Only a few minutes before she had had her doubts about it, and they had made her nervous. She was so very serious that Fuller began to look grave. But he was built of loyalty and unsuspicion; and though for a mere second a fear assailed him that the old lady was about to charge Reuben with playing his daughter false, he scouted the fancy hotly. In the warmth thus gained he spoke more briskly than common.

"Drive along, ma'am. Come to the root o' the matter."

"This letter," said Rachel, taking Ruth's answer to Reuben in both hands, "was written last night. It is addressed in your daughter's handwriting to Mr. Reuben Gold."

"Tis, yis, yis," said Fuller, impatiently, not knowing what to make of Rachel's funereal gravity.

"It appeared to me, after long consideration, that the best and wisest course I could adopt would be to bring it to you. I regard myself as being in a sense, and subject always to your authority, one of the child's natural guardians. If I did not view things in that light," the old lady explained, making elaborate motions with her lips for the distinct enunciation of every word, "I should consider that I was guilty of a sinful neglect of duty."

"Well," said Fuller, "as to sinful. But drive on, Miss Blythe."

"It appeared to me, then," continued Rachel, "that our plain duty would be to read this together, and to consult upon it."

"Wheer does the letter come from?" Fuller demanded, with a look of bewilderment.

David Christie Murray

"I discovered it in the—"

"What!" cried the old fellow, jumping from his chair and staring at her across the table with red face and wrathful eyes.

"I discovered it," replied Rachel, rising also and facing him with her head thrown back and her youthful eyes flashing, "I discovered it in the music-book which was left last night upon this table. I saw it placed there clandestinely by my niece Ruth."

"Be you mad, Miss Blythe?" asked Fuller, with a slow solemnity of inquiry which would have made the question richly mirthful to an auditor. "Do you mean to tell me as you go about spyin' after wheer my little wench puts her letters to her sweetheart? Why, fie, fie, ma'am! That's a child's trick, not a bit like a growd-up woman."

Fuller was astonished, but Rachel's amazement transcended his own.

"And you tell me, John Fuller, that you know the character of this man?"

"Know his character!" cried Fuller. "Who should know it better nor me? The lad's well-nigh lived i' my house ever sence he was no higher 'n my elber. Know his character? Ah! Should think I did an' all. The cliverest lad of his hands and the best of his feet for twenty mile around—as full o' pluck as a tarrier an' as kindly-hearted as a wench. Bar his Uncle Ezra, theer niver was a mon to match him in Heydon Hay i' my time. Know his character!" He was unused to speak with so much vigor, and he paused breathless and mopped his scarlet face with his shirt-sleeve, staring across his arm at Rachel meanwhile in mingled rage and wonder.

"His Uncle Ezra?" said Rachel, looking fixedly and scornfully back at him. "His Uncle Ezra is a villain!"

For a second or two he stared at her with a countenance of pure amazement, and then burst into a sudden gurgle of laughter. This so overmastered him that he had to cling to the table for support, and finally to resume his seat. His jolly face went crimson, and the tears chased each other down his fat cheeks. When he seemed to have had his laugh quite out, and sat gasping and mopping his eyes with his shirt-sleeve, a chance look at Rachel reinspired the passion of his mirth, and he laughed anew until he had to clip his wide ribs with his palms as if to hold himself together. A mere gleam of surprise crossed the scorn and anger of Rachel's face as she watched him, but it faded quickly, and when once it had passed her expression remained unchanged.

"Good-morning, Aunt Rachel," cried Ruth's fresh voice. "You are early." Rachel turned briskly round in time to see Ruth disappear from a white-curtained upper window. Fuller rose with a face of sudden sobriety, and began once more to mop his eyes. In a mere instant Ruth appeared at the door running towards the pair with a face all smiles. "Why, father," she cried, kissing the old man on the cheek, "what a laugh! You haven't laughed so for a year. What is the joke, Aunt Rachel?"

She saw at a glance that, whatever the jest might be, Aunt Rachel was no sharer in it.

"I know of no joke, Niece Ruth," said the old lady, with mincing iciness.

"Theer's summat serious at the bottom on it, but the joke's atop, plain for annybody to see," said Fuller. "But Miss Bly the's come here this mornin' of a funny sort of a arrant, to my thinking, though her seems to fancy it's as solemn a business as a burying."

"What is the matter?" asked Ruth, looking from one to the other. Some movement of Rachel's eyes sent hers to the table, and she recognized her own letter in a flash. She moved instinctively and laid her hand upon it.

"That's it," said her father, with a new gurgle. "'Twas your Aunt Rachel, my dear," he explained, "as see you put it somewheer last night, an' took care on it for you." Ruth turned upon the little old lady with a grand gesture, in which both hands were suddenly drawn down and backward until they were clinched together, crushing the letter between them behind her. "Her comes to me this morning," pursued Fuller, while the old woman and the young one looked at each other, "an' tells me plump an' plain as her wants t' open this letter and read it, along with me."

"Aunt Rachel!" said Ruth, with a sort of intense quiet, "how dare you?"

"I did nothing but my duty," said Rachel. "If I have exposed to you the character of these men in vain—"

"Exposed! Exposed!" cried Fuller. "What's this here maggot about exposin'? Who talks about exposin' a lad like that? The best lad i' the country-side without a 'ception!"

"You tell me then," said Rachel, turning upon him slowly, as if Ruth's eyes had an attraction for her, and she could scarcely leave them—"you tell me then that this Reuben Gold has your approval in making approaches to your daughter?"

"Approval!" shouted Fuller. "Yis. I've seen 'em gettin' fond on each other this five 'ear, and took a pleasure in it. What's agen the lad? Nothin' but the mumblin' of a bumble-bee as an old maid's got in her bonnet. A spite agen his uncle is a thing as *is* understandable."

"Indeed, sir," said Aunt Rachel, with frigid politeness. "Will you tell me why?"

"Well, no," said Fuller. "I'd rather I didn't. Look here. Let's have harmony. I'm no hand at quarrelin', even among the men, let alone among the petticuts. Let's have harmony. The wench has got her letter back, and theer's no harm done. And if theer is, ye'd better fight it out betwigst ye." With this he turned his back and waddled a pace or two. Then he turned a laughing face upon them, moving slowly on his axis. "Mek it up," he said, "mek it up. Let's have no ill blood i' the family. Nothin' like harmony."

Having thus delivered himself he rolled in-doors, and there sat down to his morning pipe. But anger and laughter are alike provocative of thirst, and seeking a jug in the kitchen he took his way to the cellar, and there had a copious draught of small beer, after which he settled himself down in his arm-chair, prepared to make the best of anything which might befall him.

The quarrel from which he had withdrawn himself did not seem so easy to be made up as he had appeared to fancy. Ruth and Rachel stood face to face in silence. To the younger woman the offence which had been committed against her seemed intolerable, and it took this complexion less because of the nature of the act itself than because of its consequences. It had mocked Reuben, and it had made her seem as if she were the mocker.

"You are angry, child!" said Rachel, at length. "I was

David Christie Murray

prepared for that. But I was not prepared for your father's acquiescence in the ruinous course upon which you have entered."

"Ruinous course?" said Ruth.

"I repeat," said the old lady, "the ruinous course upon which you have entered. These men are villains."

"Do they steal other people's letters?" asked Ruth.

"They are villains," repeated Aunt Rachel, ignoring this inquiry. "Villains, cheats, deceivers. You will rue this day in years to come." Then, with prodigious sudden stateliness, "I find my advice derided. My counsels are rebuffed. I wish you a good-morning. I can entertain no further interest in your proceedings."

CHAPTER XII

Rachel marched from the garden and disappeared through the door-way without a backward glance. The girl, holding the crumpled letter in both hands behind her, beat her foot upon the greensward, and looked downward with flushed cheeks and glittering eyes. Her life had not hitherto been fruitful of strong emotions, and she had never felt so angry or aggrieved as she felt now.

"How did she dare? What can Reuben think of me?"

These were the only thoughts which found form in her mind, and each was poignant.

A knock sounded at the street door, and she moved mechanically to answer it, but catching sight of her father's figure in the hall she turned away, and seated herself at the musicians' table.

Fuller greeted Reuben—for the early visitor was no other than he—with a broad grin, and stuck a facetious forefinger in his ribs.

"Come in, lad, come in," he said, chuckling. "I never seed such a lark i' my born days as we've had here this mornin'."

"Indeed!" said Reuben. "Can I—" He began to blush and stammer a little. "Can I see Miss Ruth, Mr. Fuller?"

"All i' good time, lad," replied Fuller. "Come in. Sit thee down." Reuben complied, scarcely at his ease, and wondered what was coming. "Was you expectin' any sort of a letter last night, Reuben?" the old fellow asked him, with a fat enjoying chuckle.

"Yes, sir," said Reuben, blushing anew, but regarding his questioner frankly.

"Was that what you took away the book o' duets for, eh?"

"Yes, sir."

"Didst find the letter?" Fuller was determined to make the most of his history, after the manner of men who have stories ready made for them but rarely.

"I don't know," replied Reuben, to the old man's amazement. "Do you know what the letter was about, Mr. Fuller?"

"Don't know?" cried Fuller. "What beest hov-erin' about? Knowst whether thee hadst a letter or not, dostn't?"

"I had a letter," said Reuben, "but I can't think it was meant for me. Perhaps I ought to have spoken first to you, sir, but I wrote to Miss Ruth yesterday—" There he paused, asking himself how to put this altogether sacred thing into words.

"Didst now?" asked Fuller, unctuously enjoying the young man's discomfort. "What might it ha' been about?"

"I wrote to ask her if she would marry me," said Reuben, with desperate simplicity.

"Ah!" said Fuller. "And what says her to that?"

"I can't believe that I have had her answer," returned Reuben, with much embarrassment. "I found a letter in the book, but I think—I am sure—it is not meant for me."

"You'll find Ruth i' the gardin," said Fuller, puzzled in his turn. "Her'll tell you, mayhap. But wait a bit; her's rare an' wroth this mornin', and I ain't sure as it's safe to be anigh her. Miss Blythe's been here this mornin'—Aunt Rachel, as the wench has allays called her, though her's no more than her mother's second cousin—and it seems as th' old creetur found out about Ruth's letter, and went and took it from wheer it was and marched it off. Her was here this mornin' t' ask me to open it and read it along with her. Theer's no tekin' note of her, Reuben, poor old ooman. Her's got a hive in her head. 'Do you know this young man's character' her says. 'Why, yis,' I says; 'it'd be odd if I didn't,' I says. 'Well,' her says, 'he's a villin.' 'Rubbidge,' says I; 'theer's no moor esteemable feller i' the parish,' I says, 'onless it's his uncle Ezra.' Then her fires up and her says, 'His uncle Ezra is a villin.' Then I bust out a-laughin' in her face. Her's flighty, you know, lad, her's uncommon flighty. Six-and-twenty year ago—it was afore thee couldst toddle—her left the parish because of Ezra."

"Because of my uncle?" There were so many things to be amazed at in this speech of Fuller's that the youngster hardly knew which to be surprised at most.

"Didst never hear o' that?" asked Fuller. "It's been the talk o' the parish ever sence her come back to live in it. Your uncle used to be a good deal at her mother's house from thirty to six-and-twenty 'ear ago, and used to tek his fiddle theer and gie 'em a taste o' music now and then. Her seems to ha' let it tek root in her poor head as he was squirin' her and mekin' up

David Christie Murray

to her for marriage; but after four or five year her got tired and hopeless, I reckon, and went away. Then I expect her begun to brood a bit, after the mode of a woman as is lonely, and has got no such thing as a man around her, and that's how it is, lad."

"My uncle!" Reuben fell to pacing up and down the room, talking aloud, but as if he addressed himself rather than his sweetheart's father. "Manzini was the last man whose works he played—the last man he ever handled bow and fiddle for. His own words. He left the book open when he went away, and closed it when he came back again." He drew the discolored note from his pocket, and stared at it with a look of tragic certainty.

"Be we all mad together?" said Fuller. "What's the matter with the lad, i' the name o' wonder?"

"I'll explain everything, sir," answered Reuben, like a man awakening from sleep. "And yet I don't know that I can. I don't know that I have a right to explain. I could ask Ruth's advice. It's hard to know what to do in such a case."

"Theer's no such thing as a straight wescut i' the house, worse luck," said Fuller. "Theer *is* a clothesline, if that 'ud serve as well."

"May I see Miss Ruth, sir?" asked Reuben. "I'll tell you all about it if I can. But I think I have found out a very strange and mournful thing."

Fuller threw open the window and called "Ruth." She came in slowly, and started when she saw Reuben there, and both she and he stood for a moment in some confusion.

"Gi'e the wench a kiss and ha' done with it," said Fuller.

"Her's as ready as thee beest willin'."

Reuben acted on this sage counsel, and Ruth, though she blushed like a rose, made no protest.

"Theer," said papa, hugging his fat waistcoat, and rolling from the room. "Call me when I'm wanted."

He was not wanted for a long time, for the lovers had much to say to each other, as was only natural. First of all, Ruth shyly gave Reuben the letter she had written the night before, and he read it, and then there were questions to be asked and answered on either side, as—Did she really love him? And why? And since when? And had she not always known that he loved her? All which the reader shall figure out of his or her own experience or fancy; for these things, though delightful in their own time and place, are not to be written of, having a smack of foolishness with much that is tender and charming.

Next—or rather interlaced with this—came Ruth's version of Aunt Rachel's curious behavior. And then said Reuben,

"I think I hold the key to that. But whether I do or not remains to be seen. I found this in Manzini. You see how old it looks. The very pin that held it to the paper was rusted half through. You see," turning it over, "it is addressed to Mr. Gold. I am afraid it was meant for my uncle, and that he never saw it. If it is a breach of faith to show it you I cannot help it. Read it, darling, and tell me what you think is best to be done."

Ruth read it, and looked up with a face pale with extreme compassion.

"Reuben," she said, "this is Aunt Rachel's handwriting. This is all her story." She began to cry, and Reuben comforted her. "What can we do?" she asked, gently evading him. "Oh, Reuben, how pitiful, how pitiful it is!"

"Should he have it after all these years?" asked Reuben. "What can it be but a regret to him?"

"Oh yes," she answered, with clasped hands and new tears in her eyes, "he must have it. Think of his poor spirit knowing afterwards that we had kept it from him?"

"It will be a sore grief for him to see it. I fear so. A sore grief."

"Aunt Rachel will be less bitter when she knows. But oh, Reuben, to be parted in that way for so long! Do you see it all? He wrote to her asking her to be his wife, and she wrote back, and he never had her answer, and waited for it. And she, waiting and waiting for him, and hearing nothing, thinking she had been tricked and mocked, poor thing, and growing prouder and bitterer until she went away. I never, never heard of anything so sad." She would have none of Reuben's consoling now, though the tears were streaming down her cheeks. "Go," she begged him—"go at once, and take it to him. Think if it were you and me!"

"It would never have happened to you and me, my darling," said Reuben. "I'd have had 'Yes' or 'No' for an answer. A man's offer of his heart is worth a 'No, thank you,' though he made it to a queen."

"Go at once," she besought him. "I shall be unhappy till I know he knows!"

"Well, my dear," said Reuben, "if you say go, I go. But I'd as life put my hand in a fire. The poor old man will have suffered nothing like this for many a day."

"Stop an' tek a bit o' breakfast, lad," cried Fuller, as Reuben hurried by him, at the door which gave upon the garden. "It'll be ready i' five minutes."

"I have my orders, sir," said Reuben, with a pale smile. "I can't stop this morning, much as I should like to."

Like most healthy men of vivid fancy he was a rapid walker, and in a few minutes he was in sight of his uncle's house. His heart failed him and he stopped short irresolutely. Should he send the letter, explaining where he found it, and how? He could hardly bear to think of looking on the pain the old man might endure. And yet would it not be kinder to be with him? Might he not be in need of some one? and if he were, who was there but his nephew—the one man of his kindred left alive?

"I'll do it at once," said Reuben, and walking straight to the door, he knocked. He would have given all he had to be away when this was done, but he had to stand his ground, and he waited a long time while a hand drew back the shrieking bolts and clattering chain within. Then the key turned in the lock. The door opened and his uncle stood before him.

"Beest early this morning," he said, with a smile. "Theer's something special brings thee here so 'soon?"

"Yes," answered Reuben, clearing his throat, "something special."

"Come in, lad," said Ezra. "No trouble, I hope. Theer's a kind of a troubled look upon you. What is it?"

Reuben entered without an immediate answer, and Ezra

closed the door behind him. The gloom and the almost vault-like odors of the chamber struck upon him with a cold sense of solitude and age. They answered to the thoughts that filled him—the thoughts of his uncle's lonely and sunless life.

"Trouble!" said the old man, in an inward voice. "Theer's trouble everywheer! What is it, lad?"

"Sit down, uncle," began Reuben, after a pause in which Ezra peered at him anxiously. "I find I must tell you some business of my own to make myself quite clear. I wrote a note to Ruth last night, and I learned from her that she had put an answer between the leaves of Manzini. I took the book home and found a note addressed to Mr. Gold. I opened it, and it was signed with an 'R,' and so I read it. But I can't help thinking it belongs to you. The paper's very yellow and old, and I think "—his voice grew treacherous, and he could scarcely command it—"I think it must have lain there unnoticed for some years."

He held it out rustling and shaking in his hand. Ezra, breathing hard and short, accepted it, and began to grope in his pockets for his spectacle-case. After a while he found it, and tremblingly setting his glasses astride his nose, began to unfold the paper, which crackled noisily in the dead silence.

When he had unfolded it he glanced across at Reuben and walked to the window.

"Theer's summat wrong," he said, when he had stood there for a minute or two, with the crisp, thick old paper crackling in his hand. "Summat the matter wi' my eyes. Read it—out." His voice was ghastly strange.

Reuben approached him and took the letter from his fingers. In this exchange their hands met, and Ezra's was like ice. He laid it on Reuben's shoulder, repeating, "Read it out."

"Dear Mr. Gold," read Reuben, "I have not answered your esteemed note until now, though in receipt of it since Thursday."

"Thursday?" said Ezra.

"Thursday," repeated Reuben. "'For I dare not seem precipitate in such a matter. But I have consulted my own heart, and have laid it before the Throne, knowing no earthly adviser.'"

There was such a tremor in the hand which held him that Reuben's voice failed for pure pity.

"Yes," said Ezra. "Goon."

"Dear Mr. Gold," read Reuben, in a voice even less steady than before, 'it shall be as you wish.'" There he paused again, his voice betraying him.

"Go on," said Ezra.

"It shall be as you wish, and I trust God may help me to be a worthy helpmeet. So no more till I hear again from you. R."

"That's all?" asked Ezra.

"That's all."

"Thank you, lad, thank you." He stooped as if in the act of sitting down, and Reuben, passing an arm about his waist, led him to an armchair. "Thank you, lad," he said again. An eight-day clock ticked in a neighboring room. "That was how it came to pass," said the old man, in a voice so strangely commonplace that Reuben started at it. "Ah! That was how it came to pass." He was silent again for two or three minutes, and the clock ticked on. "That was how it came to pass," he said again. With great deliberation he set his hands together, finger by finger, in the shape of a wedge, and then pushing them between his knees, bent his head above them, and seemed to stare at the dim pattern of the carpet. He was silent for a long time now, and sat as still as if he were carved in stone. "Who's there?" he cried, suddenly looking up.

"I am here, uncle," Reuben answered.

"Yes, yes," said Ezra. "Reuben. Yes, of course. And that was how it came to pass."

Reuben, with a burning and choking sensation in his throat, stood in his place, not knowing what to say or do.

"Wheer is it?" asked Ezra, looking up again. Reuben handed him the note, and he sat with bent head above it for a long time. "Reuben, lad," he said then, "I'll wish thee a good-mornin'. I'm like to be poor company, and to tell the truth, lad, I want to be by mysen for a while. I've been shook a bit, my lad, I've been shook a bit."

As he spoke thus he arose, and with his hands folded behind him walked to and fro. His face was grayer than common, and the bright color which generally marked his cheeks was flown; but it was plain to see that he had recovered full possession of himself, though he was still much agitated. Reuben went away in silence, and Ezra continued to pace the room for an hour. His house-keeper appeared to tell him that breakfast was on the table, but though he answered in his customary manner he took no further notice. She came again to tell him with a voice of complaint that everything was cold and spoiled.

"Well, well, woman," said Ezra, "leave it theer."

He went on walking up and down, until, without any acceleration of his pace, he changed the direction of his walk and passed out at the door, feeling in the darkened little passage for his hat.

"You sha'n't goo out wi' nothing on your stomach," said the servant, who had been watching and waiting to see what he would do. Ezra, to satisfy her, poured out and drank a cup of coffee, and then walked out into the street, bending his steps in the direction of Rachel's cottage. Twice on the way he paused and half drew from his waistcoat-pocket the yellow old note which had so long lingered on its way to him, but each time he returned it without looking at it, and walked on again.

He stood for a moment at the wicket-gate, and then opening it passed through, suffering it to fall with a clatter behind him. His hand trembled strangely as he lifted it to the door, and he knocked with a tremulous loudness. When he had waited for a time he heard Rachel's footsteps tapping on the oil-cloth of the passage which divided her toy sitting-room from her bandbox of a parlor. His gray face went a shade grayer, and he cleared his throat nervously, with the tips of his thin fingers at his month. He heard the rattling of the door-chain, but it seemed rather as if it were being put up than taken down, and this suspicion was confirmed when it was opened with a little jar and stopped short at the confines of the chain. Rachel's face looked round the edge of the door. He had time to speak but a single word—"Rachel!"

The door was vigorously slammed in his face, and he heard the emphatic tapping of footsteps as she retired. He stood for a minute irresolute, and then, quitting the porch, walked round the thread of gravelled foot-path which led to the back of the cottage. He had but rounded the corner of the building when the back door closed with a clang, and he heard the bolts shot. Next, while he still stood irresolute, he saw Rachel approach a window and vigorously apply herself to the blind cord. In the mere instant which intervened between this and the descent of the blind she looked at him with a profound and passionate scorn. The old man sighed, and nodding his head up and down retraced his steps, but lingering in the pathway in the little garden, and surveying the house wistfully, he was again aware of Rachel, who faced him once more with an unchanging countenance. This time she appeared at the parlor window, and a second time the blind came down between him and her gaze of uncompromising scorn.

"Eh, dear!" he said, tremblingly, as he turned away. "Her's got reason to think it, poor thing. It's hard to find out the ways o' Providence. If it warn't for good it couldn't ha' happened, but it's a heavy burden all the same."

CHAPTER XIII

Ezra walked home and sat there alone until evening. His house-keeper routed him from his armchair for dinner and tea, and at each meal he made a feeble pretence of eating and drinking, and, having been scolded for his poor appetite, went back to his old place. He sat there till the room was dark, scarcely moving, but wearing no very noticeable sign of pain or trouble. The story was so old, and the misfortune it related was so long past mending! He had been gray himself these many years, and the things which surrounded him and touched him had long since shared all his own want of color.

There was no relighting these old ashes. And yet, in defiance of that avowed impossibility, they seemed now and again to glow. They warmed him and lighted him back to a perception of lost odor and dead color. They stung him into some remembrance of the pain of years ago. And then, again, they were altogether cold and lifeless.

He said vaguely in a half whisper that it was a pity; and the phrase rose to his lips a hundred times—oftener than not an utterance purely mechanical, and expressing neither regret for Rachel nor for himself, nor sorrow for their division. When he was not thinking of her or of himself, he murmured that this was how it had come to pass, and did not seem to care or feel at all.

When the gloom was deepening in Ezra's ill-lighted chamber, though the light of the summer evening still lingered outside, the house-keeper came in and drew the blinds, and left behind her a single candle, which left the room as dusky as before. Shortly after this Reuben came in, and Ezra, nodding, signed him to a chair. The young man took a seat in silence.

"Well, lad," said his uncle, when to the young man the continued stillness had grown almost ponderous. The seconds had seemed to drop one by one upon him from the audible ticking of the old clock in the next room, each with an increasing weight of embarrassed sympathy.

"Well, uncle?" returned Reuben, trying to speak in his ordinary way, and only succeeding in sounding shamefully flippant and unsympathetic to his own ears.

"I've a mind to have a talk with you," said Ezra. "Is the door shut?"

Reuben rose to see, and murmuring that it was closed, resumed his seat. He waited a while in expectation that his uncle was about to confide in him.

"When beest going to make up your mind to pluck up a courage and speak to Ruth?" the old man asked.

"To Ruth, sir?" returned Reuben. The question staggered him a little.

"To Ruth," said Ezra.

"I have spoken," answered Reuben. "We are going to be married."

"That's well," the old man said, mildly. "But I looked to be told of any such thing happening. Thee and me, lad, are all as is left o' th' old stock i' this part o' the world."

"Don't think I should have kept you ignorant of it," said Reuben. "I only knew this morning. I have not seen you since till now."

"Well, lad, well," said Ezra, "I wish thee happy. But I'm sure you know that without need of any word o' mine. I asked because I meant to give out a bit of a warning agen the danger of delay. Theer's not alone the danger of it, but sometimes the cruelty of it. It's hard for a young woman as has been encouraged to set her heart upon a man, to be kept waitin' on the young man's pleasure. You see, lad, they'm tongue-tied. Perhaps"—he offered this supposition with perfect gravity—"perhaps it's the having been tongue-tied afore marriage as makes some on 'em so lively and onruled in speech when marriage has set 'em free."

There was a definite sense in Reuben's mind that the old man was not saying what he wished to say, and this sense was strengthened when Ezra, after moving once or twice in his seat, cleared his throat and began to walk up and down the room.

"Had you read that letter as you brought to me this morning, lad?" he asked, coughing behind his hand, and trying to speak as if the thing were a commonplace trifle.

"I read it because I thought that it must be addressed to me," said Reuben. "I had written to Ruth, and she told me to look in Manzini for her answer. I found nothing but that letter in the book."

"Why, how was that?" asked Ezra, without turning

towards him.

"Her own note had been taken away before I got the book." Reuben felt himself on dangerous ground. It was unpleasant to have to talk of these things, and it looked impossible to reveal Rachel's eccentricity to Ezra, knowing what he knew.

"Ah!" said Ezra, absent-mindedly. "You read the letter then!" He went on pacing up and down. "You understood it?"

"I—seemed to understand it," said Reuben. Ezra came back to his chair and seated himself with a look of half resolve.

"Reuben," he began, in a voice pathetically ill-disguised, "it was something of a cruelty as that letter should ha' been found at all after such a lapse o' time. The rights of the case was these: As a younger man than now—I was six-an'-thirty at the time—I wrote to—I wrote an offer of myself in marriage to a person as was then resident i' this parish. The day but one after I wrote I had to go up to London to see to some affairs as was in the lawyer's hands relating to thy grandfather's property. He'd been dead a year or more, and the thing was only just got straight. While theer, I heard Paganini, and I've told you, more than once, I never cared to touch a bow theerafter. I found Manzini on the music-stand and closed the pages. He was open theer as I had left him, for I was a bit particular about my things, and mother used to pretend as her dursn't lay a hand upon 'em. I waited and waited for th' answer. I met the person as I had wrote to once, and bowed to her. I've remembered often and often the start her gave, as if I'd done her some sort of insult. I could never understand how or why. I did not know as I had gi'en her any right to treat me thus contemptuous. I thought her set a value upon herself beyond my deservin's, and I abode to bear it. In the course of a two-three weeks she left the parish, and I made up my mind as her'd left despising me. I won't pretend as I might not ha' found her letter if her had been less prideful and disdainous, for in the course of a little while I might ha' gone back to the music if things had gone happier with me. But it would ha' been kinder not to know the truth at all than find it out so late."

He had spoken throughout in what was meant for his customary tone of dry gravity, but it failed him often, though for a word only. At such times he would pause and cough behind his wasted hand, and these frequent breaks in the narrative made its quiet tones more touching to the hearer than any declamation or any profession of profound regret, however eloquently expressed, could possibly have been.

"Have you explained to her since you received the letter?" asked Reuben. "Don't you think, uncle, that she ought to know?"

Ezra looked at him in a faint surprise. He supposed he had guarded himself from any suspicion of betraying his old sweetheart's personality.

"Yes," he said, still bent upon this reservation. "It happens as the person I speak of came back to Heydon Hay some time ago, and was within the parish this very day. I went to make a call upon her, and to show how Providence had seen fit to deal with both of us, but her refused to exchange speech with me. You see, Reuben," he went on, coughing with a dry mildness of demeanor, "it's doubtless been upon her mind for a many years as I was making a sort of cruel and unmanly game of her. Seeing her that offstanding, it seemed to me her valued me so lowly as to take my letter for a kind of offence. It seems now as it was me, and not her, as was too prideful."

They were both silent for a time, but Reuben was the first to speak again.

David Christie Murray

"She ought to know, uncle. She should be told. Perhaps Ruth could tell her."

"My lad, my lad!" said Ezra, mournfully reproving him. "How could I tell another of a thing like this?"

"Well, sir," Reuben answered, "I know now how the idea came into her mind, though I was puzzled at first. But she is strongly opposed to my being engaged to Ruth, and came down to tell Mr. Fuller this morning that I was a villain. I am thinking of her own lonely life, and I am sure that if Ruth and I are married she will never speak again to the only relatives she has unless this is explained. For her own sake, uncle, as well as yours, I think she ought to know the truth."

He was looking downward as he spoke, and did not see the questioning air with which Ezra regarded him.

"You know who it was, then, as wrote this letter?"

"Yes," said Reuben, looking up at him. "Ruth knew the handwriting."

"Reuben!" cried the old man, sternly. He rose with more open signs of agitation than Reuben had yet seen in him, and walked hurriedly to and fro. "Reuben! Reuben!" he repeated, in a voice of keen reproach. "Ah! when was ever youth and folly separate? I never thought thee wast the lad to cry thine uncle's trouble i' the market-place!"

"No, uncle, no! Don't think that of me," cried his nephew. "I did not know what to do. I asked Ruth's advice. I could not be certain that the note was meant for you. And—guessing what I thought I guessed—I was afraid to bring it."

"Well, well! Well, well!" said Ezra. "It's been too sad an'

mournful all along for me to go about to make a new quarrel on it. Let it pass. I make no doubt you acted for the best. Art too good a lad to tek pleasure in prying into the pain of an old man—as—loves thee. Leave it alone, lad. Let's think a while, and turn it over and see what may be done."

He went back to his arm-chair, and Reuben watched him in sympathetic silence.

"I know her to be bitter hard upon me in her thoughts," said Ezra, after a time. "The kind of scorn her bears for me is good for nobody, not even if it happens to be grounded i' the right. It might be a blow to her at first, but it 'ud be a blow as 'ud carry healing with it i' the long run. Let the wench tek the letter. It'll be easier for her to get it at a woman's hands."

He drew the cracked and faded letter from his waistcoat-pocket, and held it out towards Reuben without looking at him.

"I think that will be the best and kindest course, sir," said Reuben, accepting the letter and placing it in his pocket-book. "It may not be easy for Ruth to speak to her just at first, for she is very angry with her for having engaged herself to me."

"I have heard word of her opposing it," answered Ezra. "Theer are them in Heydon Hay as elsewheer—folks, without being aythur coarse-hearted or hard-minded, as talk of their neighbors' affairs, and love to tell you whatever there is to be heard as is unpleasing. I have been told as her describes me as a villin, and speaks in the same terms of you, Reuben. And that's why I advised you to speak out before there should be time to make mischief, if by any chance mischief might be made. And I've seen enough to know as theer's no staple so easy to mannyfacture as ill-will, even betwixt them as thinks well of each other. But, Reuben, even the best of women are talkers, and I look for it to be made a point on between Ruth and you, that no word of this is breathed except between your two selves."

"You may trust Ruth as much as you trust me, uncle," said Reuben.

"Like enough," answered Ezra. "And I've a warm liking for her. But there'll be no unkind-ness in naming my particular wish i' this affair."

"No, no," answered Reuben. "I will tell her what you say. You may trust us both."

"Let me know how things go," said the old man. "And good-night, Reuben."

A tender twilight still reigned outside, and Reuben, walking along the village street, could see the softened mass of roofs and chimneys and the dark green bulk of trees outlined clearly against the sky. The air was soft and still, and something in the quiet and the dimness of the hour seemed to bear a hint of memory or continuation of the scene which had just closed. He was going to see Ruth at once, and she was naturally in his mind, and presented herself as vividly there as if he had been in her presence. The old man's trouble was so much more real to a lover than it could have been to another man! If it were he and Ruth who were thus parted! There lay a whole heartache. He loved Ezra, and yet it did not seem possible to feel his grief half so well save by seeing it as his own. Such a lonely terror lay in the thought of parting from Ruth and living forever without her, that it awoke in him an actual pang of pain for his uncle's trouble.

"But," said Reuben, as he strode along, "that is what was. He felt it, no doubt, and felt it for many a dreary month. But it's over now, for the most part. I could have cried for him this morning, and again to-night, but it was more pity for the past than for the present."

Ezra had been a sad man always, since Reuben could remember him, and yet not altogether an unhappy one. The sunshine of his life had seemed veiled, but not extinguished. And could love do so little at its most unfortunate and hapless ending? For some, maybe, but surely not for Reuben! For him, if love should die, what could there be but clouds and darkness forever and always? But the old take things tranquilly, and to the young it seems that they must always have been tranquil. Uncle Ezra a lover? A possible fancy. But Ezra loving as *he* loved? An impossible fancy. And even six-and-thirty looked old to Reuben's eyes, for he stood a whole decade under it.

"I will go at once," said Ruth, so soon as she knew what was required of her. "I'll just tell father, and then I'll put on my hat and be ready in a minute. Will you "—with an exquisite demureness and simplicity—"will you go with me, Reuben?"

"Go and see Aunt Rachel?" cried old Fuller, when the girl had told him her intention. "Well, why not?" Ruth ran up-stairs, and Fuller waddled into the room where Reuben waited. "Ruth talks about bringin' th' ode wench back to rayson," he said, with a fat chuckle, "but that's a road Miss Blythe 'll niver travel again, I reckon. Her said good-by to rayson, and shook hands a many hears ago. It's a bit too late i' life to patch up the quarrel betwigst 'em now."

The old man's paces were so leisurely and heavy and Ruth's so quick and light that she was in the room before he had formulated this opinion, and stood at the looking-glass regarding Reuben's reflection in its dimly illumined depths as she patted and smoothed the ribbons beneath her chin.

"Let us hope not, father," she said; and then turning upon Reuben, "I am ready."

He offered her his arm and she took it. It was the simple fashion of the time and place. No engaged lovers took an airing of a dozen yards without that outward sign of the tie between them. They walked along in the soft summer evening, pitying Ezra and Rachel in gentle whispers.

"I was thinking just now if you and I should part, dear—if their case were ours!"

"Oh, Reuben!"

And so the grief of the old was a part of the joy of the young, tender-hearted as they were. They played round the mournful old history.

"But you would speak, Reuben? You would never let me go without a word?"

"And if I didn't speak, dear? If something held me back from speaking?"

"But you wouldn't let it hold you back."

"Not now, darling. But I might have done yesterday—before I knew."

Before he knew! He must have always known! But of that she would say nothing.

In front of the one village shop in which the pair of window candles still glimmered, they paused, while Reuben searched his pocket-book for the note, and then went on again, in perfumed darkness, until they reached the gate of Rachel's cottage.

"Be brave, darling," Reuben whispered here. "Don't let her repulse you easily."

Ruth entered at the gate, stole on tiptoe along the gravelled path, knocked and listened. The whole front of the little house was in darkness, but by-and-by even Reuben from his post behind the hedge heard the faint noise made by slippered feet in the oil-clothed hall. "Who's there?" said' a voice from within.

"Dear aunt," Ruth answered, "let me in. Do, please, let me in. I want to speak to you."

Reuben, listening, heard the sound of the jarring chain, and the door was opened. He peeped through the interstices of the hedge, and saw Miss Blythe smiling in the light of the candle she carried in her left hand.

"Dear niece," said Rachel, with an unusually fine and finicking accent. "Enter, you are welcome."

Ruth entered, the door was closed, and Reuben sat down on the bank outside to await his sweetheart's return.

"I understand," said Rachel. "You are welcome, my child. I detest rancor in families. I can forgive and forget." As she spoke thus she led the way into her small sitting-room. To Ruth the poor creature's unconsciousness seemed terrible. She laid her arms about Aunt Rachel's withered figure, and cried a little as she leaned upon her shoulder. "There, there," said Aunt Rachel, with a note of patronage in her voice, "compose yourself, dear child, compose yourself. I am glad to see you. Take your own time, dear child, your own time."

At this Ruth cried afresh. It was evident that Aunt Rachel supposed her here to perform an office of penitence; and it was all so pitiful to the girl's heart, which, tender enough by nature, had been made soft and more tender still by her recent talk with Reuben in the lane.

"Don't talk so. Don't speak so," she said, brokingly. "Dear aunt, read this, and then you will know why I am here."

"Ah!" sighed Aunt Rachel, with a world of meaning. "What did I tell you, my dear?" She took the letter from her niece's hand, kissed the charming bearer of it casually, as if in certainty that she would soon be comforted, and began to search for her glasses.

Ruth, understanding the old lady's error, was moved still more by it, but emotion and tender interest were at war, and she sat in a half frightened silence, piteously wondering what would happen. Rachel had found her glasses, had set the letter upon the table before her, and now drawing the candle nearer, placed the spectacles deliberately astride upon her fine little nose, snuffed the candle, and took up the cracking old bit of paper with an air of triumph and hope fulfilled which cut Ruth to the heart.

The younger woman hid her face in her hands, and furtively watched the elder through her fingers.

Rachel read but a line, and then dropping the letter stared across the candle at Ruth, and passed a hand across her forehead, brushing her glasses away in the act. She groped for them, polished them with an automatic look, and began again. Ruth, too frightened even to sob, still looked at her, and save for the rustle of the withered paper in the withered fingers the silence was complete.

"What is this?" cried Aunt Rachel, suddenly. "Why do you bring me this?" She was standing bolt upright, with both hands clasped downward on the letter.

"It was only found last night," said Ruth, rising and making a single step towards her. "From the hour you wrote it until then it was never seen. Reuben found it and brought it to me."

The old maid's face went white, and but that the chair she had thrust away from her in rising rested against the mantle-piece, she would have fallen. Ruth ran towards her and set a protecting arm about her waist. Her own tears were falling fast, and her voice was altogether broken. "It was in Manzini, the book you took Reuben's letter from. He found it there, and thought it came from me, until he saw that the paper was old, and that it did not quite answer his own letter. He took it to his uncle Ezra, and the poor old man's heart is broken. Oh, aunt, his heart is broken! He had never seen it. He had waited, waited—"

She could say no more, she was so agitated by her own words, and so stricken by the stony face before her.

Suddenly the old maid melted into tears. Reuben, sitting and waiting on the bank of the hedge without, had heard Ruth's broken voice, and now he could hear Rachel weeping. The night was without a sound, and he could hear nothing but the murmurs and sobbings from the little sitting-room. Rachel cried unrestrainedly and long, and Reuben waited with exemplary patience. At last Ruth came out and whispered to him,

"Tell father I am going to stay with Aunt Rachel to-night."

Reuben, naturally enough, would have kept her there and questioned her, but she ran back into the cottage before he could detain her, and after lingering a while bareheaded before the casket which held her, he took his way back to Fuller and gave him his daughter's message.

"Ah!" said Fuller. "At that rate it 'ud seem to be pretty well straightened out betwigst 'em. I'm glad to think it, for theer's nothin' like, harmony among them as is tied together. But hows'ever her an' the wench may mek it up, Reuben, thee'lt be a villin till the end o' the chapter." The villany attributed to Reuben and Ezra tickled the old man greatly, and his fat body was so agitated by his mirth that his legs became unequal to their burden. He had to drop into his great cushioned arm-chair to have his laugh out. "That villany o' thine 'll be the death o' me," he said, as he wiped his eyes.

Rachel and Ruth sat far into the night, and the old maid told over and over again the story of the courtship and the misunderstanding between herself and Ezra.

"Even when he was young," she told her listener often, "he was shy and proud. And he would think I had treated him as though he had been the dirt beneath my feet. I did. I did. He will never forgive me. Never, never."

She always cried afresh tempestuously at this, but when the first passion of her grief had worn itself out she came back to her story and lauded Ezra without stint. He was proud, oh yes, he was proud, but then it was not in a way to hurt anybody. He joined in the sports of the other young men when she was quite a girl, a mere chit of a thing, my dear, and he was master of them all. Then Ruth chimed in. And so was Reuben now. Reuben was not like the rest of them. He was their master in everything, and everybody who was old enough to remember said that he was more like his uncle than like his father even. The duet of praise, accompanied by the old maid's tears, murmured along for an hour.

"You will meet him now?" Ruth suggested, rather timidly. "You will be friends again?"

"We could never bear to meet each other," cried Rachel. "How could I come before him?" Then, "I must go away."

"No, no," Ruth pleaded, "you must not go away. You must stay here. You must be friends again. What shall we tell him, dear? He has found the letter at last, and he sends to you. Can you let him think that you are still against him?"

"No," said Rachel, almost wildly. "You will tell him I went away because I could not bear to see him. I ought to have known him too well to have thought so basely of him."

"It was his duty to speak to you. It was less your fault than his. It was nobody's fault. It was a disaster." Ruth thought poorly of Ezra's tactics as a lover, but she was not bent on expressing her own opinions. Reuben would never have acted in such a way. He would have known at least whether his letter had been received or no. Would any *man* take silent contempt as a final answer from the woman he loved? It was the man's real business to come conquering, whatever airs of gentleness he might wear. And animated by these reflections the girl became filled with impatience at the old maid's self-upbraidings. She was sorry, sorry with all her heart, for both, but if there were fault at all it lay on Ezra's side. "I shall see him in the morning," she said, finally, thinking of Reuben. "He will go to his uncle."

"Child," said Aunt Rachel, with the beginning of a return to her old manner, "do you think I can consent to have my affairs bandied from messenger to messenger in this way? I will write."

She said this boldly enough, but her heart shrank from it. Her mind went blank when she tried to figure what she should say. She could do nothing but prostrate herself anew before the re-established idol. She began to realize the fact that whatever disguise of hate and despite her love had taken, she had done nothing but love him all along.

Ruth contented herself with the promise, but, as it happened, Rachel never wrote, or had need to write, upon this question. For Reuben, strolling early in the morning, and finding his feet wandering in the direction of Rachel's cottage, encountered his uncle, and their talk rendered the letter unnecessary. Ezra flushed and coughed behind his hand in more than a commonly deprecatory way when he sighted his nephew.

"Well, lad," he began.

"Ruth took the letter," answered Reuben. "I waited outside for her, and I know Miss Blythe was deeply affected by it, because I heard her crying. Ruth stayed all night with her," he continued, "and I suppose"—with a flush and a little hesitation—"I suppose she's there now."

"That means as they two are reunited?" said Ezra; and, without saying much more, the old man took his nephew's arm and they strolled by the cottage together.

Its inmates were early astir despite the lateness of the hour at which they had retired; and hearing voices as they stood together in the bedroom renewing the moving duet of the evening, they peeped through the curtains and saw uncle and nephew go by arm-in-arm. At this they flew together and embraced, and from that moment the duet became broken and confused. The little maid who assisted Rachel in her household affairs had not jet arrived; so the old lady herself lit the fire and made tea, while Ruth established herself in ambush in the parlor, and kept a watch upon the road. When Rachel came in to lay the snowy table-cloth, the china and the spoons made an unusual clatter in her trembling hands, and the two were in such a state of agitation that breakfast was a pure pretence. While they were seated at table Reuben and Ezra again strolled by; and Ruth divined the fact that not only was Reuben waiting for her, which was to be expected, but Ezra was attending the moment when she should quit the house in order that he might make a call upon Aunt Rachel. So in such a state of tremulous-ness as she had never experienced before—even when she took Reuben's note from the pages of Manzini or hid her own there—she arose, and, protesting that her father would never breakfast in her absence, and that she should be roundly scolded for being so late, she put on her hat and gloves, kissed Aunt Rachel's cold cheek, and ran out into the lane with blushes so charming and becoming that she might have been taken for the very humanized spirit of the dawn, lingering an hour or two beyond her time to make acquaintance with daylight. If this simile should seem to border on the ridiculous, the responsibility of it may be safely thrown upon Reuben, who not merely met her with it in his mind, but conveyed it to her as they walked homeward together. Ezra was even more bashful than Ruth, though in him the sentiment wrought less attractive tokens of itself.

"I'll walk about a little while farther," he said, awkwardly, when he had bidden Ruth good-morning; and without need to watch him, they knew that he had walked no farther than Rachel's cottage. The girl, on leaving it, had neglected to close the door, and the old maid had not dared to rise. He stood in the open door-way, and it gave him a mute invitation to enter, though he had not courage to accept it. He knocked faintly once or twice, and by-and-by was aware of a

174   David Christie Murray

movement in the parlor. He turned towards the door and saw it open slowly, and Rachel looked out at him, trembling from head to foot, with signs of tears in her face.

"Miss Blythe," he began, shakily, "I trust all ill-feelin' is at an end between us. May an old friend exchange a word with you?"

"Pray come in," said Miss Blythe, in a frightened whisper; and he entered. "Will you take a seat?" she asked him.

"Rachel," he said, "I was to blame, but never as you thought. But I kept single for your sake, Rachel."

By what wonderful alchemy of nature the withered heart grew young again at that moment, Heaven knows; but it was out of a heart suddenly impassioned and warm with youth that she answered him,

"And I will keep single for yours."

CHAPTER XIV

Ferdinand, in obedience to the call of the political situation, had absented himself from Heydon Hay for a week or two. The Liberals had put into the field a stronger man than he had expected to encounter, and there was a sudden awakening in the constitutional camp. He had to go the rounds and visit his bandsmen, and without being particularly alert himself to see that everybody else was on the *qui vive*. The constitutional candidate was, perhaps, as little interested in the coming strife as any man in the limits of the constituency, but he had allowed himself to be entered for the race, and was bound to a pretence of warmth even if he could not feel it. Ruth was not much in his mind while he was away, but when he came back again he found time once more hanging heavy on his hands; and being greeted by her when he went to listen to the quartette party precisely as he had been from the first, he determined more than ever to start a pronounced flirtation with the haughty little hussy, and bring her to a proper sense of her position. So he went early to church afoot on Sunday morning, leaving his lordship to follow alone in his carriage, and he chatted affably with the members of the little crowd that lingered about the lich-gate and the porch, and there awaited Ruth's coming.

Fuller was rather impressed with the young man's civility as a general thing, being open to the territorial sentiment, and

David Christie Murray

was proud to be singled out from the rest by the Earl of Barfield's visitor, and publicly talked to on terms of apparent equality. And Ruth, who accompanied her father, was on this particular morning not quite what she had been hitherto. "When Ferdinand raised his hat and proffered her his hand she blushed, and her eyes held a singular uncertainty he had never before remarked in them. He could even feel in the few brief seconds for which her hand lay in his own that it trembled slightly. Aha! She began to awake, then. The young Ferdinand plumed himself and spread himself for her vision. The old man, not unwilling that his neighbors should remark him in familiar intercourse with the great of the land, lingered at the porch, and for once Ruth did not desert his side and run into the church alone.

"Upon my word," said Ferdinand, "there is something in the air of Heydon Hay, Mr. Fuller, which would seem to be unusually favorable to the growth of feminine charms. May I congratulate Miss Ruth upon her aspect this morning?"

He meant the little thing no harm. He could compliment her in her father's presence as easily as out of it, and perhaps with a better conscience. Whensoever loosed from the string the arrow of compliment would find its mark. Besides, the very carelessness of his appreciation would help its force. He might be a little kinder and more confidential later on.

"Well, sir," said Fuller, with a chuckle, "her's bound to look her best just now."

"Father," said Ruth, with an amazingly sudden vivacity, "I want to speak to you. Excuse us, Mr. De Blacquaire."

Her face was of the color of the rose from brow to chin, and her eyes were as shy as ever in spite of her vivacity. They met Ferdinand's smiling, conquering glance for a moment, and no more. He raised his hat and withdrew. He had shot his arrow, and had hit the white. He could afford to retire contented for the moment, and he did so. But by-and-by that young Gold, who played first fiddle in the quartette, came up with his auburn mane, with his fiddle tucked under his arm, and stopped to talk with Ruth and Fuller. Ferdinand, exchanging a friendly word or two with a doubtful voter, watched with interest. She was blushing still, and still surveying the ground, and marking patterns on it with the toe of her pretty little boot—conscious of his glance, the puss, no doubt, and was posing a little for his admiration.

Ferdinand sat in the Barfield pew, and Ruth sat opposite. Why, the philtre was working more and more! She was so conscious that she seemed scarcely able to raise her eyes; and when, as happened no less than three times, she met his glance, she looked down in the sweetest confusion. The victorious young gentleman was so absorbed in his own reflections that he took but little note of the service, and suffered his attention to it to be for the most part mechanical. But on a sudden a certain quite indefinable sense of general interest touched him. Something was doing, or was going to be done, which was not altogether in the common.

"I publish banns of marriage," said Parson Hales, in those generous old port-wine tones of his, "between Reuben Gold, bachelor, and Ruth Fuller, spinster, both of this parish, and—"

Mr. Ferdinand de Blacquaire realized with a shocking suddenness and vividness that he was an ass and a puppy. He learned later on that he was not absolutely either, but he gets a twinge out of "I publish banns of marriage," even unto this day.

Sennacherib, who sat near Reuben in the music-gallery, nudged him with his elbow.

"Knowest what's what?" he whispered, to the younger man's prodigious scandal and discomfort. "Hast got the best wench i' the parish."

Reuben would willingly have chosen another time and place for the receipt of congratulations.

Both Rachel and Ezra were in church, and each looked seriously and sadly down, thinking of what might have been.

When service was over the ringers met by previous arrangement, and startled Heydon Hay with a peal. Ezra was at Rachel's side when the flood of sound descended on them and drowned his salutation. But they shook hands, and walked away side by side until they reached the front of Ezra's house, when Rachel turned to say good-by.

"I'll walk a little way if you'll permit it, Miss Blythe," said Ezra; and the old maid assenting, they walked on until the strenuous clang of the bells was softened into music. "They'll mek a handsome couple," said Ezra, breaking the silence.

"Upon acquaintance with the young man," said Rachel, "I discover many admirable qualities in him." The speech was prim still, and was likely to continue so, but it had lost something, and had gained something. It would be hard to say what it had lost or gained, and yet the change was there, and Ezra marked it, and thought the voice tenderer and more womanly. Perhaps the flood-tide of youth which had swept over her heart at their reconciliation had not entirely ebbed away, and its inward music lent an echo to her speech. If it were there still, it was that which lent some of its own liquid sweetness to her look. Not much, perhaps, and yet a little, and discernible.

There were half a dozen homeward-going worshippers ahead

of them, a hundred yards away, and a handful more a hundred yards behind, as Ezra's backward glance discerned. They were all moving in the same direction, and at pretty much the same pace. The air was very quiet, and the clear music of the bells made no hinderance to their talk.

"I'm thinkin', Miss Blythe," said Ezra, slowly, walking with his hands clasped behind him and his downcast eyes just resting on her face and gliding away again, "I'm thinkin' as the spectacle of them two young lives being linked the one with the other gives a sort of a lonely seeming to the old age as you and me has got to look to."

"Perhaps so, Mr. Gold," said Rachel, stopping with dry brevity in her walk and holding out her hand. "I must hasten homeward. I wish you a good-morning."

Ezra took her proffered hand in his, shook it gravely, and accepted his dismissal.

Not many newspapers came to Heydon Hay, and the few that found their way thither reached the regular subscribers a day or two after their news was stale to London readers. Ezra got his *Argus* regularly every Tuesday morning, and in fine weather would sit in the garden to read it. It happened that on the Tuesday after the first time of asking of the banns, he sat beneath a full-leaved, distorted old cherry-tree, gravely reading "Our Paris Correspondence," when his eye fell upon an item of news or fancy which startled him and then set him a-thinking. "All Paris," said our correspondent, "was delightfully fluttered by the approaching marriage of the Marquis of B. and Madame De X. Madame De X. was a reigning beauty in the days of the Consul Plancus. It would be unfair to reveal her precise age even if one knew it. The Marquis of B. was turned seventy. The two had been lovers in their youth, and had been separated by a misunderstanding. The lady had married, but the gentleman for her sake had kept single. Monsieur X. had lived with his bride for but a year, and had then succumbed to an attack of phthisis. Now, after a separation of forty years, the two lovers had met again, the ancient misunderstanding had been romantically explained, and they had decided to spend the winter of their days together. Paris was charmed, Paris was touched by this picture of a life-long devotion presented by the Marquis of B."

Ezra, rising from his seat, laid the paper upon it and walked soberly about the garden. Then he took up the journal, surrounded the paragraph which related to the devotion of the Marquis of B. with heavy ink-marks, waited patiently until the lines dried, folded up the paper, put it in his pocket, and walked into the road. There he turned to the left, and went straight on to Miss Blythe's cottage. There in the garden was Miss Blythe herself, in a cottage bonnet and long gloves, busily hoeing with little pecks at a raised flower-bed of the size of a tea-tray. She looked up when Ezra paused at the gate, nodded with brisk preciseness in answer to his salutation, and then went on industriously pecking at the flower-bed.

"My weekly paper has just arrived, Miss Blythe," said Ezra. "It appears to contain an unusual amount of interestin' matter, and I thought I'd ask you in passing if you'd care to have a look at it."

"You are remarkably obliging, Mr. Gold," said Rachel. "I thank you extremely." She took the newspaper from his hand and retired into the house with it. Ezra lingered, and she returned to resume her occupation.

"It is beautiful weather," said Ezra.

"It is beautiful weather, indeed," said Rachel. Ezra lingered on, but rather hopelessly, for she would not so much as glance in his direction so far as he could see, but her features were entirely hidden by the cottage bonnet.

"I trust you will find a item or two as will be of interest," he said, after a lengthy pause. Rachel contented herself with an emphatic-seeming little nod at the flower-bed. "Good-day, Miss Blythe."

"Good-day, Mr. Gold, and thank you very much for being so good as to think of me."

They did not encounter again until the following Sunday morning, when the banns between Ruth and Reuben were called a second time. The ringers were at work again when Ezra and Rachel met in the porch as the church-goers streamed slowly away, and the two shook hands mutely. They walked on side by side until Ezra's house was reached, and neither spoke until then. Pausing before the door, Miss Blythe put out her hand.

"If I might be allowed to go a little farther, Miss Blythe," said Ezra, gently. Rachel withdrew her hand and said nothing. So once more they walked, apart from other home-going worshippers, down the lane that led to Rachel's cottage.

"Did you," began Ezra, pausing to cough behind his hand— "did you tek a look at the paper, Miss Blythe?" He received a nod for sole answer, unless the pinching of the lips and an unconsciously affected maiden drooping of the eyelids might be supposed to add to it. "Did you happen to read a particular item," said Ezra, pausing to cough behind his hand again, "a item in the letter from Paris?"

"Really, Mr. Gold," said Rachel, marching on with

exceeding stateliness, and looking straight before her, "at our ages that piece of news would offer a very frivolous theme for conversation."

"Might we not talk of it without being frivolous, Miss Blythe?" asked Ezra.

"Decidedly not, in my opinion," Miss Blythe responded.

"To talk of love," pursued Ezra, glancing at her now and then, "in the sense young people use the word, between persons of the ages of that lady and gentleman, 'ud be frivolous indeed. But I persoom, Miss Blythe, they did not talk so."

"I should think not, indeed," said Rachel, with decision. "I should hope not."

"But to talk of love as love is betwixt the elderly—to talk of companionship—to talk of shelterin' one another again the loneliness of late old age—to talk of each one tekin' up the little remnant of life as was left to 'em and putting it i' the other's hands for kindly keepin'! Should you think as that was ridiculous, Rachel?"

"I should think," said Rachel, "that old fools are the greatest fools of all." Ezra sighed. "I do not know," she said at this, "that the poor-marquis is so much to blame, but the lady should have known better than listen to his folly."

"I had thought," said Ezra, patiently, "you would ha' took a different view of it, Rachel." They went on to the gate without another word. "Good-morning, Rachel," Ezra said there. "Don't be afraid of me. I will not come back again to this subject. I had hoped you would not ha' looked on it with such mislikin'; but sence you do, I will say no more about it."

So they parted, and met again and were good friends, and not infrequent companions, and Ezra said no more.

The eve of Reuben's great day came round, and Reuben was dismissed from his sweetheart's presence to wander where he would, for Ruth and her assistants (among whom was none more important than Aunt Rachel) had a prodigious deal to do. The lovers were to leave directly after their marriage for no less a place than London, and there were dresses to be tried on and finished and packed, and altogether the time was trying. In his wanderings about the fields Reuben encountered the younger Sennacherib, whom he strove vainly to avoid; not because he disliked him, but because his own thoughts kept him in better company just then than the younger Sennacherib was likely to provide in his own person. But Snac was not a man to be lightly shaken off, and Reuben bent himself to listen to him as best he might.

"So," said young Sennacherib, "thee beest goin' to enter into the bounds of 'oly matterymony?" Reuben laughed, and nodded an affirmative. "Well, theest done a very pretty thing for me amongst you."

"For you?" said Reuben. "How?"

"Why this way," said Snac, bending his knees to make the tight embraces of his cords endurable. "Thee wast by when my feyther gi'en me the farewell shillin'. Very well. I'd got nothin' i' the world, and he knowed it. After a bit he begun to relent a bit, though nobody 'd iver had expected sich a thing. But so it was. He took to sendin' me a sov a week, onbeknownst to anybody, and most of all to mother. Well, mother sends me a sov a week from the beginning unbeknownst to anybody, and most of all him. Her'd ha' gone in fear of her life if her'd ha' guessed he knowed it. And now my income's cut down to half, and all because of this here weddin' o' thine."

"I don't see how," said Reuben.

"Why thus," said Snac, with a somewhat rueful grin. "This here Rachel Blythe as has come back to the parish has come to a reconciling with your uncle, as was a by-gone flame of hern; and her tells my mother as it's thee and thy bride as browt that to pass."

"True enough," Reuben allowed; "but still I don't see—"

"An' niver will see," said Snac, "till thee lettest me tell thee. Her comes to my feyther's house, this Miss Blythe, an' tells mother what a beautiful thing this reconcilin' is, and they fall to weepin' and cry-in' to my feyther both together, an' all on a sudden, t' everybody's mightiest astonishing, what's he to do but say, 'Theer, I forgi'en him. Hold your jaw, the pair on you!' Well, now, see what a pitch I'm let to fall on. Feyther durn't tell mother for his life as he helped me; her durn't tell him as her helped me. So they mek up their minds to gi'e me a pound a week betwigst the two on 'em, and that's how it comes about with these here cussed reconcilings, as I'm done out o' fifty per cent, o' my income. Look here, Mr. Gold, don't you goo about reconcilin' no more of my relations."

"Why, Snac," cried Reuben, "it's none of my doing."

"Well," Snac allowed, "it'd be hard upon a man to mek him answerable for all the doin's of his wife's mother's second cousin. But if it had been a man as had ha' done it, I'd ha' had a try to punch his head for him. I should ha' took a trial trip at you yourself, Mr. Gold, for all so big and all so handy as you be."

"Well, Snac," said Reuben, "it will be all the better for you in the end, and I hope it may mend sooner. But if the fact of my meaning to get married has done so much good as you say it has, I'm very glad to know it, and I'll take it as a happy sign."

It seemed an augury of happiness as he walked alone about the fields, and dwelt upon it. It seemed a fitting thing that love should spread peace abroad, and that peace should multiply itself.

On the morrow the ringers rang; and being inspired by plenitude of beer and rich gratuity, and hearty good-will into the bargain, they rang till sundown. And when the wedding was over, and the bride and bridegroom had driven away with cheers and blessings in their train, the wedding-guests sat in the garden with the sylvan statues standing solemnly about, and the bells making joyful music. Everybody was very sober and serious when the excitement of cheering away the wedded pair was over, and in a while the guests began to go. Ezra and Rachel lingered among the latest, and Rachel's going was the signal for Ezra to say his good-bys and follow. She made no objection to his society, and they walked on without speaking. The declining sun shone full in their faces, and cast their shadows far behind. Except for themselves the lane was lonely.

"Did you see in last week's copy of the *Argus*," said Rachel, suddenly, and with great dryness, "that the Marquis of B. and the lady are united?"

"I noted it," said Ezra. "Do you think so badly of them as you did?"

Rachel said nothing.

"Do you think so badly of them as you did?" he asked again, and still Rachel said nothing. The lane was lonely. He laid a hand upon the shoulder nearest him, and asked the question for a third time. Still she said not a word, but bent her head, perhaps to avoid the level sunlight. "Shall we garner up the years that are left for us together, dear?"

She gave no answer still, but he seemed to understand. They walked on side by side towards the sunset, and the joy-bells, half sad with distance, sounded in their ears.

THE END

Choose from Thousands of 1stWorldLibrary Classics By

A. M. Barnard
Ada Leverson
Adolphus William Ward
Aesop
Agatha Christie
Alexander Aaronsohn
Alexander Kielland
Alexandre Dumas
Alfred Gatty
Alfred Ollivant
Alice Duer Miller
Alice Turner Curtis
Alice Dunbar
Allen Chapman
Alleyne Ireland
Ambrose Bierce
Amelia E. Barr
Amory H. Bradford
Andrew Lang
Andrew McFarland Davis
Andy Adams
Angela Brazil
Anna Alice Chapin
Anna Sewell
Annie Besant
Annie Hamilton Donnell
Annie Payson Call
Annie Roe Carr
Annonaymous
Anton Chekhov
Archibald Lee Fletcher
Arnold Bennett
Arthur C. Benson
Arthur Conan Doyle
Arthur M. Winfield
Arthur Ransome
Arthur Schnitzler
Arthur Train
Atticus
B.H. Baden-Powell
B. M. Bower
B. C. Chatterjee
Baroness Emmuska Orczy
Baroness Orczy
Basil King
Bayard Taylor
Ben Macomber
Bertha Muzzy Bower
Bjornstjerne Bjornson

Booth Tarkington
Boyd Cable
Bram Stoker
C. Collodi
C. E. Orr
C. M. Ingleby
Carolyn Wells
Catherine Parr Traill
Charles A. Eastman
Charles Amory Beach
Charles Dickens
Charles Dudley Warner
Charles Farrar Browne
Charles Ives
Charles Kingsley
Charles Klein
Charles Hanson Towne
Charles Lathrop Pack
Charles Romyn Dake
Charles Whibley
Charles Willing Beale
Charlotte M. Braeme
Charlotte M. Yonge
Charlotte Perkins Stetson
Clair W. Hayes
Clarence Day Jr.
Clarence E. Mulford
Clemence Housman
Confucius
Coningsby Dawson
Cornelis DeWitt Wilcox
Cyril Burleigh
D. H. Lawrence
Daniel Defoe
David Garnett
Dinah Craik
Don Carlos Janes
Donald Keyhoe
Dorothy Kilner
Dougan Clark
Douglas Fairbanks
E. Nesbit
E. P. Roe
E. Phillips Oppenheim
E. S. Brooks
Earl Barnes
Edgar Rice Burroughs
Edith Van Dyne
Edith Wharton

Edward Everett Hale
Edward J. O'Biren
Edward S. Ellis
Edwin L. Arnold
Eleanor Atkins
Eleanor Hallowell Abbott
Eliot Gregory
Elizabeth Gaskell
Elizabeth McCracken
Elizabeth Von Arnim
Ellem Key
Emerson Hough
Emilie F. Carlen
Emily Bronte
Emily Dickinson
Enid Bagnold
Enilor Macartney Lane
Erasmus W. Jones
Ernie Howard Pie
Ethel May Dell
Ethel Turner
Ethel Watts Mumford
Eugene Sue
Eugenie Foa
Eugene Wood
Eustace Hale Ball
Evelyn Everett-green
Everard Cotes
F. H. Cheley
F. J. Cross
F. Marion Crawford
Fannie E. Newberry
Federick Austin Ogg
Ferdinand Ossendowski
Fergus Hume
Florence A. Kilpatrick
Fremont B. Deering
Francis Bacon
Francis Darwin
Frances Hodgson Burnett
Frances Parkinson Keyes
Frank Gee Patchin
Frank Harris
Frank Jewett Mather
Frank L. Packard
Frank V. Webster
Frederic Stewart Isham
Frederick Trevor Hill
Frederick Winslow Taylor

Friedrich Kerst
Friedrich Nietzsche
Fyodor Dostoyevsky
G.A. Henty
G.K. Chesterton
Gabrielle E. Jackson
Garrett P. Serviss
Gaston Leroux
George A. Warren
George Ade
Geroge Bernard Shaw
George Cary Eggleston
George Durston
George Ebers
George Eliot
George Gissing
George MacDonald
George Meredith
George Orwell
George Sylvester Viereck
George Tucker
George W. Cable
George Wharton James
Gertrude Atherton
Gordon Casserly
Grace E. King
Grace Gallatin
Grace Greenwood
Grant Allen
Guillermo A. Sherwell
Gulielma Zollinger
Gustav Flaubert
H. A. Cody
H. B. Irving
H. C. Bailey
H. G. Wells
H. H. Munro
H. Irving Hancock
H. R. Naylor
H. Rider Haggard
H. W. C. Davis
Haldeman Julius
Hall Caine
Hamilton Wright Mabie
Hans Christian Andersen
Harold Avery
Harold McGrath
Harriet Beecher Stowe
Harry Castlemon
Harry Coghill
Harry Houidini

Hayden Carruth
Helent Hunt Jackson
Helen Nicolay
Hendrik Conscience
Hendy David Thoreau
Henri Barbusse
Henrik Ibsen
Henry Adams
Henry Ford
Henry Frost
Henry James
Henry Jones Ford
Henry Seton Merriman
Henry W Longfellow
Herbert A. Giles
Herbert Carter
Herbert N. Casson
Herman Hesse
Hildegard G. Frey
Homer
Honore De Balzac
Horace B. Day
Horace Walpole
Horatio Alger Jr.
Howard Pyle
Howard R. Garis
Hugh Lofting
Hugh Walpole
Humphry Ward
Ian Maclaren
Inez Haynes Gillmore
Irving Bacheller
Isabel Cecilia Williams
Isabel Hornibrook
Israel Abrahams
Ivan Turgenev
J. G.Austin
J. Henri Fabre
J. M. Barrie
J. M. Walsh
J. Macdonald Oxley
J. R. Miller
J. S. Fletcher
J. S. Knowles
J. Storer Clouston
J. W. Duffield
Jack London
Jacob Abbott
James Allen
James Andrews
James Baldwin

James Branch Cabell
James DeMille
James Joyce
James Lane Allen
James Lane Allen
James Oliver Curwood
James Oppenheim
James Otis
James R. Driscoll
Jane Abbott
Jane Austen
Jane L. Stewart
Janet Aldridge
Jens Peter Jacobsen
Jerome K. Jerome
Jessie Graham Flower
John Buchan
John Burroughs
John Cournos
John F. Kennedy
John Gay
John Glasworthy
John Habberton
John Joy Bell
John Kendrick Bangs
John Milton
John Philip Sousa
John Taintor Foote
Jonas Lauritz Idemil Lie
Jonathan Swift
Joseph A. Altsheler
Joseph Carey
Joseph Conrad
Joseph E. Badger Jr
Joseph Hergesheimer
Joseph Jacobs
Jules Vernes
Julian Hawthrone
Julie A Lippmann
Justin Huntly McCarthy
Kakuzo Okakura
Karle Wilson Baker
Kate Chopin
Kenneth Grahame
Kenneth McGaffey
Kate Langley Bosher
Kate Langley Bosher
Katherine Cecil Thurston
Katherine Stokes
L. A. Abbot
L. T. Meade

L. Frank Baum	Paul G. Tomlinson	T. S. Arthur
Latta Griswold	Paul Severing	The Princess Der Ling
Laura Dent Crane	Percy Brebner	Thomas A. Janvier
Laura Lee Hope	Percy Keese Fitzhugh	Thomas A Kempis
Laurence Housman	Peter B. Kyne	Thomas Anderton
Lawrence Beasley	Plato	Thomas Bailey Aldrich
Leo Tolstoy	Quincy Allen	Thomas Bulfinch
Leonid Andreyev	R. Derby Holmes	Thomas De Quincey
Lewis Carroll	R. L. Stevenson	Thomas Dixon
Lewis Sperry Chafer	R. S. Ball	Thomas H. Huxley
Lilian Bell	Rabindranath Tagore	Thomas Hardy
Lloyd Osbourne	Rahul Alvares	Thomas More
Louis Hughes	Ralph Bonehill	Thornton W. Burgess
Louis Joseph Vance	Ralph Henry Barbour	U. S. Grant
Louis Tracy	Ralph Victor	Upton Sinclair
Louisa May Alcott	Ralph Waldo Emmerson	Valentine Williams
Lucy Fitch Perkins	Rene Descartes	Various Authors
Lucy Maud Montgomery	Ray Cummings	Vaughan Kester
Luther Benson	Rex Beach	Victor Appleton
Lydia Miller Middleton	Rex E. Beach	Victor G. Durham
Lyndon Orr	Richard Harding Davis	Victoria Cross
M. Corvus	Richard Jefferies	Virginia Woolf
M. H. Adams	Richard Le Gallienne	Wadsworth Camp
Margaret E. Sangster	Robert Barr	Walter Camp
Margret Howth	Robert Frost	Walter Scott
Margaret Vandercook	Robert Gordon Anderson	Washington Irving
Margaret W. Hungerford	Robert L. Drake	Wilbur Lawton
Margret Penrose	Robert Lansing	Wilkie Collins
Maria Edgeworth	Robert Lynd	Willa Cather
Maria Thompson Daviess	Robert Michael Ballantyne	Willard F. Baker
Mariano Azuela	Robert W. Chambers	William Dean Howells
Marion Polk Angellotti	Rosa Nouchette Carey	William le Queux
Mark Overton	Rudyard Kipling	W. Makepeace Thackeray
Mark Twain	Saint Augustine	William W. Walter
Mary Austin	Samuel B. Allison	William Shakespeare
Mary Catherine Crowley	Samuel Hopkins Adams	Winston Churchill
Mary Cole	Sarah Bernhardt	Yei Theodora Ozaki
Mary Hastings Bradley	Sarah C. Hallowell	Yogi Ramacharaka
Mary Roberts Rinehart	Selma Lagerlof	Young E. Allison
Mary Rowlandson	Sherwood Anderson	Zane Grey
M. Wollstonecraft Shelley	Sigmund Freud	
Maud Lindsay	Standish O'Grady	
Max Beerbohm	Stanley Weyman	
Myra Kelly	Stella Benson	
Nathaniel Hawthrone	Stella M. Francis	
Nicolo Machiavelli	Stephen Crane	
O. F. Walton	Stewart Edward White	
Oscar Wilde	Stijn Streuvels	
Owen Johnson	Swami Abhedananda	
P.G. Wodehouse	Swami Parmananda	
Paul and Mabel Thorne	T. S. Ackland